Content Marketing:

*Proven Strategies to Attract
an Engaged Audience Online
with Great Content and
Social Media to
Win More Customers,
Build your Brand and
Boost your Business*

Gavin Turner

outlined in this book.

By reading this document, the reader agrees that under no circumstances is the author responsible for any losses, direct or indirect, which are incurred as a result of the use of the information contained within this document, including, but not limited to, —errors, omissions, or inaccuracies.

Table of Contents

Conclusion

Introduction:

The world nowadays has never been this associated with information and engagement focused on a target audience. According to a recent Nielsen Total Audience Report, almost half of an adult's day in the U.S.is spent on consuming content.

Think about it for a second: that's over 11 hours each day!

Now add this to the fact that newer platforms for content consumption are being utilized at a rapid pace.

The potential for selling products and services through the use of effective content is where opportunities abound where businesses big and small alike can thrive. Where the problem lies, however, is the failure to leverage this opportunity fully.

And although the content is being published consistently by some companies, it is being done just for the sake of pumping out as much content as possible, without much planning or purpose for their customers and losing sales in the process.

This is where Content Marketing comes in.

What Content Marketing Is

Content marketing can be explained as creating and sharing content like videos, social media posts, and blogs to market the products and services of a brand.

A few examples of where Content Marketing is being used:

1. eBooks

2. Whitepapers

3. Videos

4. Infographics

5. Images

6. Press Release

Many companies have utilized content marketing at its par. For example, Hubspot, Coca Cola, McDonald's, Hootsuite, and more! Just adding content is not useful by itself, so these companies understood their need to engage with their customers innovatively.

Publishing content with the purpose to make

sales

Now content can be easily understood as a material or piece of information that is produced to market your business. This content is the key to developing a relationship with customers. The content can take any form. For example, brand images, videos, social media messages, text on a website, or webinars. Various types of content are being read and watched by a lot of customers every day. But, only a couple of brands are getting noticed and followed regularly. Even you can be one such brand, a brand that visitors can trust. When your brand is getting noticed in terms of great content, there are assured chances that these visitors can become your regular buyers. By implementing the strategies in this book, you can get noticed by your target audience. This book is a one-stop-shop to educate you about effective content marketing and how it can be a boon for your brand so that you can engage with your customers.

Numerous brands are doing content marketing because it is a sort of trend. Almost every niche of business utilizes content marketing, without actually knowing the role of it. They perceive content marketing as just a method of creating content. But this is far from the truth! Creating content is only a part of content marketing. Setting up a proper content strategy is as essential as creating the content itself. When your content speaks for itself, you can be sure that it reaches the right audience at the right time. The real purpose of content marketing is to indulge your ideal customers with your business. When your customers are getting satisfied with your content, they tend to know you better. The search engine bots are not only crawling your content - but your customers consume it. Content marketing is all the buzz right now, with a ton of interest, energy, and passion currently going into it. There are a lot of people nailing this, getting it right and seeing massive results from their content marketing, but there are also a lot of people who are failing miserably.

The solution to delivering content that sells

So what is the solution? The solution is setting up an effective content marketing plan for the business, and this plan is outlined in this book.

Content marketing is an act of *owning* the content. The content marketing is done in a way that a set of visitors or customers can be easily targeted for your brand. The most favorable content is *consistent* content. If you're consistent and reliable for your audience, they will reward you with steady sales. According to a survey published on mobile e-commerce, almost 80% of users shop through e-commerce. Thus, it is quite evident that you can breakthrough your business via content marketing. If you're using Yoast on WordPress and utilizing YouTube and blogging, you can rest assured that you will rank better in the search engine results. For whatever key terms you want, you should be optimizing your content to really be using a content marketing strategy to reach its optimal potential, and then promoting your content on all the best-suited platforms. So, when you have a new video that comes out on YouTube it should be being published on Instagram, it should be linked on Facebook, you should talk about it on LinkedIn or Snapchat or wherever else your audience hangs out.

The bottom line is: You should be promoting your content! Because if you have everything set up the right way, when someone comes across your content, they will love you and will want to buy from you. They will feel compelled to go down the rabbit hole of figuring out who you are and what you are about, and they come out the other end a dedicated and loyal customer. So promote it all you can--because you never know where someone's going to lay eyes on it. We use content marketing as a channel because we can make a meaningful and measurable impact on our business. We don't do this because it's sexy, we don't do it because it's cool, we don't do it because renowned companies are doing it. We do it because it *works*. Through this book, I will explain the exact step-by-step process on how to understand what content marketing is and how it works--and how to make it work for *you*.

This book lets you know about which things a business has to share with its customers and how to use content effectively, and what exactly makes it a successful content marketing campaign. Working actively in this industry for several years, I know that content portrays the middleman between your business and your consumers. I have handled many niches and products, and so through this book, I will be sharing my insights for an in-depth dive in Content Marketing, which has helped many business owners to reach their customers effectively.

Content marketing is information with a purpose; in simple words; everything you post or share leads to a series of information that is being passed on to your customers to make a sale. In this case, you have no other option but to share only relevant content to your customers. Irrelevant content leads to a decrease in current customers, let alone finding new ones. What happens when your customers are not getting the information they need? They start searching for other sources to get that information. And what if you don't know who your actual customer is? There is an entire chapter in this book about how to know your target audience. Thus, this book is going to be your best resource if you want to know everything about content marketing.

How do you learn what to post, when to post, and where to post? All of these things can be a huge issue if you don't understand what content marketing is in actual. If your posts are getting a lot of likes, comments, followers, etc., then you are making content marketing work, but if your content helps to spread a positive message among the customers, then you have got content marketing doing your work for you. A bunch of likes, comments, and followers doesn't guarantee success, but your customer engagement *does*. You must be prepared to engage deeply with your customers through your content.

Well-created content ensures the success of your business in any industry. If your content doesn't reflect your brand, it is not useful. Good content reflects your business and its vision and mission. As far as business is concerned, everything is content. A small social media post, an eBook, a video, or an image; everything consists of content. Want to spread brand awareness? You need content. Want to educate your customers? You need content. Thinking of reaching more customers? You need content. So, when everything revolves around content, whether it is a website or social media, you definitely need a better content marketing plan at hand. If you avoid integrating proper content marketing tactics, you can lose a substantial number of customers.

Now, bear in mind that content marketing may not be for everyone. Not every business is going to thrive even through meticulous targeting through content marketing. However, if you can measurably impact your business in a positive way with content marketing, you need to go for it. If your content marketing effort is not getting you many clients, it can lead you to better content creation. If one content strategy doesn't work, you may apply another. This strategy leads you to a series of better customer acknowledgment action. And thus, your business starts a journey towards success. Content marketing may not be appropriate for every business, but fortunately, many businesses boom when they make effective use of content marketing channels--mostly because it compels the user to *do* something. To avoid facing this loss, you can try implementing content marketing tips and tricks mentioned in this book.

So, in a nutshell, content marketing is, at its core, the act of throwing all of your eggs into the content basket and letting that basket market your products or services for you. Content marketing is, in essence, the strategy of using content--including text, audio, video, or social media posts--for the purpose of marketing.

Any business can use content marketing at any stage of the company. From product to service to infopreneur, content marketing is effective in every field because it can both attract your customers and engage them at the same time. The content you're putting out is acting as the way that people get to know you; they don't have to come into your store or call you. Your content is letting them learn about you quicker and more efficiently. If you are creating a product or service or you're teaching, this allows you and your business to make a positive impression on people.

Wondering how that works? There are plenty of deep insights in this book, where you will be willing to get up and act on your content. There are many useful topics like how to reach the ideal audience, how to create the ultimate piece of content, and more! I recommend you read this book from Chapter 1 to the very end because it will create a whole new outlook on content marketing and its various methods.

The strategies you are about to read include:

- Content Marketing
- Content Monetizing
- Social Media Marketing
- Targeting Audience
- Engaging the Audience
- Content Creation
- Content Marketing Strategies

- Content Marketing Plan
- Content Marketing Calendar

And more!

This book covers valuable information to have a successful content marketing strategy set up for your business. It doesn't matter if you're a beginner or a pro at content marketing; there is an abundance of information about the topic in this book.

To reach your consumers, read this book, and apply the quick action steps as often as you can. These steps are quick guides on what you should do to boost your content marketing efforts. It takes you from the basics of content marketing to the advanced strategies that can be applied immediately. So read on and reap the benefits today.

Chapter 1: Getting Started with Content Marketing

Chapter 1: Getting Started with Content Marketing

1.1 What is Content Marketing?

"Content marketing is the only marketing left." - *Seth Godin*

According to this quote, content marketing is the only medium through which a business can interact with its customers, because, in this modern era, you cannot depend on traditional (and some might say outdated) marketing mediums. Since pretty much everyone uses various social media platforms, you can get in touch with your consumers through a website or other social media outlets.

Content is widely used by traditional marketers to attract customers. The content is a primary resource used to increase awareness of any brand and build brand reputation. Many businesses shifted their focus towards content in the 19th century.

In the year 1732, Benjamin Franklin published *Poor Richard's Almanack* with the purpose of brand promotion.

In 1801, bookstore Librairie Galignani used content marketing by featuring articles from famous authors of the era.

In the year 1861, Samuel Wagner launched the *American Bee Journal,* a popular magazine that is being published even now.

In 1867, Hartford Steam Boiler Inspection and Insurance Company started *The Locomotive,* the oldest magazine published in the United States.

The Edison Electric Lighting Company Bulletin used content marketing to inform people about the benefits of electricity in 1882.

Then in 1887, Charles Scribner's sons started publishing *Scribner's Magazine,* wanting to portray the lives of the most famous authors of the magazine.

Johnson & Johnson launched the *Modern Methods* publication in 1888. Its emphasis was on antiseptic wound treatment and targeted toward doctors who needed sterile bandages.

Top Content Marketing Companies

Accenture Interactive

PwC Digital Services

IBM

Dentsu

1.2 Why is Content Marketing Important?

Why does content marketing matter?

Here are seven reasons to show content marketing is the future of online business.

1. The first reason content marketing is crucial to your business's success is that your business is unique. You cannot write fitness content if you're running a SaaS company. So, your content is what takes you to the customers. There is evidence that the growth of a website can be boosted 7.8 times by using content marketing tactics.

2. The second big reason is that it generates massive goodwill in the marketplace. So if you land on a website and it has a product listed on it, and you find yourself unsure of what the product is or what its purpose is, you're not going to want to buy that because you have no idea what it is all about. However, if they're always asking and answering questions instead of always

asking customers to buy stuff, then they're actually providing great value and good content to the viewers over time. What's happening is they're shifting the relationship with the consumer--instead of being the business that is always just asking for a sale, now they are being viewed as an entity that is adding the value to their lives.

3. The third reason is that providing great content is probably the easiest way to achieve effective marketing other than if you have an amazing product. Top-notch content is the best way to generate word-of-mouth, so the content ends up getting shared. In today's world, online social media runs the game, and if you're providing content that is valuable to other people, they will spread the word among others. When you're reading stuff or creating videos, think about is this valuable in the sense of making people say to themselves, "Wow, this is amazing! I need to share this!" That is the new currency in the online business arena. If the content is amazing, and it serves your audience, then it will spread almost without any effort (or control) on your part, which is pretty cool.

4. The next big reason is that content marketing is key

for drawing online business. It attracts the right people to your business while repelling the wrong people away doing business with you. It effectively targets your business's market while whittling away those outside of your target audience. Let's take videos as an example, and consider the tendency for people to make split-second judgments when presented with any given media. When you publish your content by posting videos, others are making judgments like, "I don't like this guy; his product would be useless to me." On the other hand, they might make judgments like, "Wow! - this is what I've spent my whole life waiting for, and now someone is offering it for sale. How can I buy this service?" It may sound counterintuitive, but it's a win-win situation for your business. The wrong people filter themselves out, while the right people gravitate toward your product. Your business is not a one-size-fits-all solution for everybody, and that's okay.

5. The fifth reason is that content marketing helps to lower resistance for people to do business with you. We are not in the business to sell iPhones; we are not Apple, we are not IBM--we're not these massive brands that people know. You can build a great brand, but you have to be incorporating that with some type of value-

added to the marketplace. So you need to provide content in a way that speaks to people's problems and helps to solve them over time. You develop that relationship through your content, which is marketing your business for you. As you build a relationship with your target audience, even virtually, the barrier gets lower and lower, and the audience becomes more likely to buy your stuff and become a loyal customer, which is as crucial as it is ideal.

6. The sixth reason why content marketing is of utmost importance in today's age is that Google values content above all else. So Google "thinks" about this and is constantly ranking websites based on whether other people are deeming these websites to be important or irrelevant.

7. The seventh reason that content marketing is powerful is that it is evergreen. If your content is evergreen, it can keep working for you for years to come as long as it also remains relevant. If you are providing that kind of relevant, evergreen content, you are giving your audience answers over and over again, and that has a major impact--both on the audience and your business--because you're getting your ideas out

into the marketplace and providing actionable solutions to your audience.

1.3 How Content Marketing Works

If you have a business and you're using the internet to market it via social media outlets, blog posts, videos or podcasts--in other words, via content published online--that is content marketing. Content marketing is creating a piece of content to share, either online or in another venue (it doesn't *have* to be the internet, even if most content marketing is done online). The internet is usually the medium that a lot of people frequent, and then there are other mediums within that, but the point of content marketing is the same as any other form of marketing: to attract and retain clients.

A lot of people's brains stop at the word "content" when they think about content marketing; for them, their idea of content marketing is just posting blogs, making tweets, and publishing videos. However, content marketing is much more than that. Content marketing is creating value for the potential customer, client, or possible audience. A lot of us might be creating content for just ourselves, content that appeals specifically to us, because we're not thinking all the way to the end of the equation. It's about what the client values, but it's also about getting value back.

So, how are we creating content? How is it applicable to someone's life? How is our content making them want to do something active? How is our content instilling an emotional feeling--something that gets them to share with their community? That's the part of content marketing that starts to pay you back for what you have put into it. Content marketing doesn't work for you when you just put some videos or blog posts or social media posts out there into the ether and leave it at that. You have to get that value back for it to serve a purpose for you, and to do what is necessary to make your audience *want* to get connected to your content.

Content and Marketing

Your content is the backbone of your content marketing strategy. It can be in any form, but the primary purpose of your content is to provide valuable information.

After the content, the next step is to strategize marketing. Your content cannot reach your customers without appropriate marketing methods. These may include, emails, ads, or search engines. Though it is true that content marketing takes time to show results, many businesses become impatient. They often declare their content marketing strategy a big fail and give This is the biggest mistake! Go up and beyond your content and marketing strategy, to see what gives you results and what drives you nuts.

How to produce content that sells and persuades?

1. Firstly, identify the topic on which you have to create the content.

2. Then do extensive research on that topic and collect the information about that topic.

3. After that, decide on which medium you need to post that content.

4. Talk to your team! Meet your team and ask for their opinions about each part of the content.

5. Finally creating the actual content.

6. Then promote it.

Content marketing works in different stages as follows:

1. Strategy – This is the most crucial phase in content marketing, where most of the businesses fail. A robust content marketing strategy starts with – your potential customers, then digging deep into who your competitors are, how you can stand above them, researching topics that aren't already covered by your competitors and how to create better experiences for the customers than them.

How strategy works

You can have a look at your competitors by searching your business-related keywords on search engines. These rankings can give you an idea what kind of content you can create for your customers to rank above your competitors. There are many tools like AHREFS and SEMrush that can be used for this purpose.

Then research in even greater depth and analyze what kind of a post this is and how they are promoting it. You can use RSS to download their content and then use tools like SimilarWeb and SEMrush to follow these promotions.

After this step, brainstorm ideas about what topics are *not* being used by your competitors. If they are doing it through blogs, try making videos, and so on. You have to make sure your every step is taking you to your ideal customers.

2. Content Creation – Done with your strategy? The next part is to create the content. These days, content creation and designing go hand-in-hand. So make sure you can invest in both because it is hard to appeal to the customers in this competitive environment.

The content creation process can be implemented as explained below:

Plan – You must engage in planning about when to publish the content and how to promote it.

Ideation – You can create the most effective content by combining data-driven research and creativity.

Draft and Completion – Create the first draft of the executed idea, and after getting feedback, create the second draft, and then finally complete the content.

3. Promotion – To many people, promotion is a bit hard to understand and to apply. Content promotion is not just publishing the content or putting the posts to auto-publish mode. For effective content promotion, you must have a compelling idea, a brilliant design, shareable content, and multi-platform content, e.g., a video.

Most businesses are afraid of doing content promotion because they tend to believe that it is too much. But I kid you not; you must promote your content because of the following reasons:

The first reason is your regular visitors or your loyal customers. These customers are continuously engaging with your social media posts, blog posts, or video comments. They want to interact with your brand, so promote your content for their sake.

The second reason is your research. If you have created a piece of content in the first place, then it must be relevant to a lot of readers. People are asking questions, or they have doubts, which ultimately must be answered by your brand.

The third reason is communication. Your customers are looking for real people to talk to. They need to feel appreciated by humans, not by robots. So promote your content as much as possible.

4. Measurement – The fundamental reason behind doing content marketing is having a purpose. That purpose can be anything like getting followers, getting traffic, or getting sales. Once you know the purpose, start tracking and measuring the results you are getting out of your content marketing strategy. Gear up your Google analytics account, set up goals, measure the amount of traffic you're getting and set up custom dashboards and reports. This measurement and tracking can give you an idea of how your content is performing at various platforms.

5. Realignment – After everything has been done, realign your strategy with your goals. Look deep into how your content is attracting your customers and what aspects are those you need to improve.

Keep on repeating these steps from 1 to 5 to keep the buzz among your customers going. These steps can make the content rank better in the search engines, and you can interact with your customers at a personal level.

Effective content marketing has to inform or entertain right away. It can't just be bullet points or demands that customers shell out money. The business has to add value to get that value back in return. Consumers respond well to this form of marketing, and this positive response helps businesses to thrive.

Your Quick Start Action Step:

Several useful resources can demonstrate how content marketing works for your business. Visit these helpful sites to learn more:

https://www.thinkwithgoogle.com/intl/en-ca/marketing-resources/content-marketing/

https://www.reddit.com/r/ContentMarketing/

https://contentmarketinginstitute.com/2015/01/advice-web-content-strategy-matt-cutts/

https://www.quicksprout.com/6-steps-to-your-first-content-marketing-plan/

Chapter 2: How Content Marketing Drives Sales

Chapter 2: How Content Marketing Drives Sales

Content marketing can be done using both free and paid methods, but did you know you can also generate a few bucks of your own through content marketing? This method is called content monetization. You can earn money when you create content, when it gets clicked or when it gets shared (for example, by adding affiliate links to blog content). This monetization of your content can be a plus when it comes to the content marketing efforts of your business.

2.1 How Can Content Marketing Help a Business?

The goal of content marketing is to attract and engage your ideal audience and to get them to buy your product or service. Now, the typical customer will ask themselves a few questions on the path to purchasing a product or service from you. To start, they may ask themselves whether they even *need* a product like yours or whether they should keep continue doing what they're doing and scroll past it. If they decide that they need to make some changes, they'll want to know what solutions are accessible on the market and what criteria differentiates your product or services from the various options--for example, pricing. Once they gain that understanding, they'll want to evaluate the different options (including yours) and learn more about how your product or service stacks up concerning the criteria that matter the most to them. If your product or service becomes a favorite, they'll want to validate their decision before they finally make their purchase.

So, where does content marketing come into this? The goal of content marketing is to give your potential customers the quality information they need on their path to purchasing your product. For example, when they're deciding if they need to make a change, you can show them a video that explains the benefits of adopting the kind of product or service that you provide. Alternately, you could show them an infographic that outlines how many companies use this type of solution and how they've benefited from it to help them gain a better understanding of which types of solutions are available to them. You could offer them an industry white paper or maybe an eBook to tell them about your particular solution and why it's their best option. You could show them a presentation and a competitive feature grid, and when they're almost ready to commit to you but need a little more validation, that's when you can share some case studies and testimonials. And that is how you can make content marketing work for your business.

Sales Funnel and Content Marketing

Let's dig deeper into what a good content marketing framework looks like for you if this is something you're looking to invest in. The best content marketing is used at every step of the funnel. So, for example, if you've set up your sales funnel, you know how it works, first comes your buyer persona or your customer avatar, and then you have other phases of the funnel, and you can use content marketing for each step of the funnel that's clearly defined. So in a nutshell, the content marketing can be used for each phase of the funnel.

So let's get to the funnel. The top of the funnel has the customer awareness phase, next to or middle funnel is the consideration phase; the bottom funnel is the conversion phase. Once you have converted that user, you are looking at monetization, retention, and loyalty.

Let's talk about the top of the funnel: awareness. The things we might be doing would be acquiring new visitors and segmenting them accordingly. The middle funnel involves driving visitors back to the site, getting them to come back two, three, four, or more times. The bottom part of the funnel is where we convert them with our core offer, and then monetization and retention are getting users to buy again and again and making sure they're happy advocates of the business.

There are many examples of the content marketing funnel, which will outline to lend a thorough understanding.

Top Funnel Content - The first step is awareness, and it is the top of the funnel content. Some of the content that we could create for our content marketing strategy at the top of the funnel might be blog posts, which might be videos. It could be podcasts or social media posts. The metrics we might monitor for these things might be traffic or maybe inbound links to that content.

Middle Funnel Content - All of the stuff we would do for people in the middle funnel might be lead magnets, or asking for an email address in exchange for a freebie, it might be tools, or downloads, or webinars. The metrics we might be monitoring could be pixels, email list growth or email campaign click-through rate, or tripwire conversion rate.

Bottom Funnel Content - This could be something along the lines of a free trial offer. This, of course, depends on your business to a certain extent--but a free trial, a tripwire, kind of a low-dollar product, or maybe a webinar of a 30-minute call, or something such as, "Click here to book a free consultation." Our metrics here might be our core-offer conversions, or it could be your email campaign click-through rate or average order value, maybe something like our user lifetime value--all of these are metrics you might monitor for the bottom funnel content.

To sum this all up, content marketing is when the advertiser is the one creating the content, and the content and advertising are blended into one. You could have content marketing at every phase of the funnel, and you're going to need to monitor different metrics along the way, moving each user down to every stage of the funnel for your content marketing strategy.

2.2 Content Monetizing

Content monetization is simple: it is the act of earning some cash while you're doing your content marketing. The first step towards content monetization is generating content--because you can't monetize without content. Another thing that is essential to monetizing content is having a large customer base, or at least having content that has the potential to generate more traffic.

Methods to monetize content marketing:

- Social Media Marketing - Having many followers over social media platforms can get you to the shore of SMM, or Social Media Marketing. You can create your business profile over Facebook, Twitter, Instagram, etc., and then share content that is relevant to your business. That content can direct consumers to your website or product. Thus, this method can provide you with a massive spike in sales.
- Email Marketing - Emails are a traditional means of getting connected to the customers. Emails can never go wrong when it comes to content marketing. You can create an email campaign that is engaging and clear, and it should have a call to action at the end. Create an email marketing campaign today if you don't have one in place already.
- Search Engine Optimization - This is the most

profitable marketing strategy that is being used today. You, too, can experience the benefits of SEO and get your website ahead of the game and ahead of the websites of your competitors. This process is all about optimizing your website to get a better ranking in search engines, such as Google.

- PPC (Google Adwords) - This tried-and-tested method has been available for a while, and it can be extra useful for a new startup. You can set up sponsored ads that appear in Google search results and add a quick call to action along with your ad. The call to action could be anything that gets the person clicking to connect with you, such as your phone number, your website link or your product listing page.

- Affiliate Marketing - Remember how we talked about adding affiliate links to blog content earlier? This form of marketing helps to connect your business with well-established companies, who can affiliate your product on their websites (and vice versa). This sort of marketing can generate quick traffic and consistent money.

- Paid Posts - For this type of content

monetization, you can reach other businesses in your niche to write paid posts about your website. This type of post can help you get quick traffic, and it can spread the word about your business's story.

- Videos - If nothing else works, videos can be your best friend. You can create informational videos at YouTube and monetize it to get visitors gravitating toward your website. You can create ads for your YouTube channel, and they can be shown to others who are conducting searches related to your topic. The more views your videos have, the more you can earn.

2.3 How Content Marketing Drives Sales

Content marketing is one of the most significant parts of sales funnels. Effective content marketing takes effort, but that effort quickly pays off, and that is why it is crucial to start off with this before you build any of your other sales funnels. Let me explain how that works: Let's take the example of blogging, as blogs are one of the most common types of content marketing out there. Let's say you have a blog. Now, most people just put up a blog post and say to themselves, "Okay, this is for SEO, or this is for traffic, or this is for thought leadership." That is just the very bare-bones minimum that can be done to take this random piece of content and turn it into a part of content *marketing*.

Your content marketing sales funnel is your front-line sales funnel. Picture this: You have a chessboard. You have the pawns that go out, in the beginning; they do all of the hard work in the first part of the game. These pawns are just like your content marketing sales funnel--they are always the first pieces to move. They may not be used much in the end game, but they are crucial in the beginning. So when it's about your content marketing sales funnel, the purpose of it is to essentially build you and your business up as an authority by providing value and building trust in your marketplace and with your potential customers.

Before people opt-in to start one of those sales funnels, whether it's a webinar funnel, a launch funnel, or a book funnel--whatever type of funnel it is, it is critical to build some level of trust or authority before people feel comfortable providing their name or email address to go through that sales funnel process. That's where your content marketing sales come in, and this is what tips a lot of people off to your content marketing. The sales funnel doesn't necessarily sell a product or service; it serves to lend authority and credibility to your business and to the product or service that you offer.

Content marketing has a few requirements to be effective. It has to solve a particular problem that's related to a sales funnel in your business. And of course, your sales funnel is associated with a product or service. This is going to get a little tricky, but bear with me--I promise that this is going to make sense and at the end, your product or service will sell. So, how does this actually work? Your blog post talks about how to solve a problem, and then at the end of the blog post, the call to action is to take the first step into a sales funnel. The call to action at the end of the post can either involve a content upgrade or have an opt-in or offer at the bottom of the blog. This is where you say to the audience that they can get this PDF version of the blog or they can get this cool free tool or free video that is related to what the blog was talking about, either significantly or marginally. The good thing is that your content marketing sales funnels usually are only a couple of steps long. Since the purpose of the content is to sell a front-end free offer on one of your sales funnels, it serves as the foundation of your sales funnel marketing.

Your content marketing sales funnels are created in a way that takes on the first pillar of sales funnel design: indoctrination and value delivery. So your content should be 100 percent value, which serves to build trust and build a relationship with people who haven't ever heard of you before. Once they have consumed that piece of content then you offer them, the first step is an actual sales funnel on your back end. So your content marketing sales funnels are only designed to drive traffic to your other sales funnels that influence people and provide more value to sell your products and services. Now, the big warning red flag I have for this content marketing process is to keep in mind that you want to ensure that whatever problem the customer had that your product or service solved is always consistent and harmonious throughout your process. Therefore, every piece of content you have as part of your marketing sales funnel needs to solve a specific issue that does not conflict with the problem that your product or service solves.

Your Quick Start Action Step:

The following are some interesting informational resources about the process of content monetization:

https://ducttapemarketing.com/monetize-content/

https://www.shopify.com/partners/blog/content-monetization

https://skimlinks.com/blog/content-monetization-explained/

Chapter 3:
The Right Mindset in Using Content to Break Through the Noise

Chapter 3: The Right Mindset in Using Content to Break Through the Noise

3.1 The Right Mindset to Create Content

Apart from creating, posting, and sharing content, content marketing provides a strategic approach to the entire process of marketing as a whole. All of these things can only be achieved by going in the right direction. You must be able to think positively and strategically about your content. Using an effective content marketing strategy can take your business to the next level so that you can achieve success. An effective content marketing strategy involves a set of steps to take to create a roadmap of how to create and publish your content. Ranging from searching relevant information to engaging positively with customers and generating sales, your content marketing strategy helps you identify both the boons and pain points of your content marketing efforts.

3.2 The Importance of the Right Mindset

Why is a strong content marketing strategy so

important to your brand, and why does mindset matter so much? The importance lies in the need to be in front of people all the time; you want to be in front of your potential customers, driving value. To deliver value today, you have to be providing useful content. You have to think about how you can learn from any bumps there may be in the road along the way, rather than taking a defeatist mindset. Content is available on all kinds of different platforms: Facebook, Instagram, your blog, your website--there are just so many different places where content can be made available and utilized to drive sales. So, you need to think critically about where your customers are, and how you can deliver value through a strong content marketing strategy.

3.3 How to Implement the Right Mindset with Content Marketing

Do you know that to set up a content marketing strategy, you need to have the right mindset? And that mindset should be that of a publisher. When you think like a publisher, you have full control over your content. You act and think as if your content is significant for your organization and your brand. After all, your content is an essential medium to reach your customers.

There are many methods to implement the right mindset with content marketing:

1. Grab attention - Instead of holding attention, think about how to grab users' attention. It could be anything like an image, blog post, or a social media post. You have to create content that attracts your customer's attention. One practical way to grab attention is to invest in paid ads.

2. You're the owner of your content - If you think and shift your mindset to this crucial point, you will feel empowered. The more responsible you are for your content, the more powerful your content strategy will be.

3. Don't avoid social media - If you're taking social media marketing for granted, then you're making a big mistake. Social media is as vital as other content. It's crucial to interact with customers through social media.

4. Blog - If you need quick and dedicated traffic, implement blogging on your website. A blog can be informative and engaging at the same time.

5. Prioritize marketing before creating content
- If you think that you should create content first, then think about marketing. You're going in the wrong lane. Just like publishers, start marketing your topics on your social media even before creating that blog post. It creates a sense of curiosity in your visitors.

Your Quick Start Action Step:

Utilize your keywords and start making changes to your content. The best way to become successful in business is to have the right mindset and the right plan. So plan your content marketing and get ready to see your success in the coming days. Go for it!

Chapter 4: Aligning Your Content with Your Brand

Chapter 4: Aligning Your Content with Your Brand

4.1 Aligning Content with Brand

Content marketers must employ strategy to properly align their content resources to the goals of the business. A brand strategy is the allocation of people's money and time in the pursuit of profitable growth. On the other hand, a content marketing strategy needs to reflect what your business is. An effective content marketing strategy ensures that we allocate the resources efficiently to drive revenues when you utilize the approach by building up the buyer preference for the company's products.

Content creation sits inside the framework of brand identity, so you've got to create good content to draw the buyer in. It should be done through strategic alignment and not just in the context of sales and marketing.

A well-known brand requires its message to be delivered to its customers. Thus, the best way to do so is through content marketing. You can adjoin your brand's stories to the content marketing plan. It is the most effective method of making your customers aware of what you offer and how you offer it.

The ideal brand strategy should focus on buyer personas. You must be willing to strategize how your brand collaborates with your content through appropriate copywriting at the initial stages of your business set up.

Your mission, values, and vision must be directly proportional to the idea that solves the problems of your customers.

Make sure you tell your base who you are and what you truly believe when you are building the foundations of your brand strategy as well as content marketing strategy. Sincerity builds trust.

The key to the perfect strategy alignment is to speak the language of your business when you are doing content marketing posts.

Get your taglines ready to spark the customers' enthusiasm. The taglines are the hooks to pull customers towards your business, so make sure they are on point.

4.2 Importance of Aligning Content with Brand

You do need to align your content with both your brand and your prospects. A thriving brand has three key ingredients - it's useful, unique, and aligned. Now, by "aligned," I mean that there's a balance created by the brand between the brand's content and the customers.

There are several important aspects of aligning content with the brand:

• If the content gets imbalanced on either side, you've got trouble. Suppose the content is all about promotions. This type of content is not helpful to the customers for assisting them with achieving their goals--or worse; you are not able to sell your products to your customers. This is because you are pushing your content to sell and not to engage the audience. So there has to be some balance between your content, your business goals, and customer queries.

• Now in the case of direct selling at a store, it's apparent that you need to convince the customer to buy your product. But as far as online sales are concerned, you have to be careful at your content selection. It has to be knowledgeable and useful and valuable, and at the same time, it has to deliver the message about your brand.

- You can be an imbalanced on the prospect side as well, by creating content that is solely focused on the customer's attention. This, in turn, makes you lose any connection with your brand and its goals. So, you have to be careful about your content creation to make it aligned with the brand.

How do you create content which is balanced as well as aligned with the brand? The best advice is to imagine your content as a bridge between your brand and your customers.

Start with the goals of your business, whether they are to build brand awareness, or reputation management, or launching your product and solutions to the customers. After reviewing these goals, put yourself into your customer's shoes. Think about what they need from you and what their obstacles might be, and work from a perspective of addressing those issues and needs. When thinking about creation, make sure you keep your content aligned with your business's motives and customer's needs. Ask yourself how this piece of content is relevant to your business. Why should it matter to your prospects; what does it do for them? That's the content development bridge, and when you build it correctly and with care, your content starts working for you.

4.3 How to Align the Content with the Brand

1. Know About Your Customers -The first method to aligning the brand with content is to think about the customers and their needs. Many brands are just bragging about themselves, and that's the wrong approach. Prioritize your customers at every turn and every step along the way. By doing so, you will solve many marketing issues right out of the gate.

2. Focus On Your Business's Values - The best marketing strategy is to improve your values as a business. When you know not only how and what you are serving to your customers, but why you are serving it, it becomes easier to create useful, valuable content marketing posts.

3. Empower Your Readers - Every time a user visits your website, they need to be experiencing a sense of empowerment. Make sure your content encourages them to move on to the next stage. The content must be valuable enough to them to empower them to feel like

they can rely on your business.

4. Consider UX - The user experience is the keynote of what your content is delivering to the outside world about your business. You can ask your visitors about how they feel at the end of your content piece and provide them a means of expressing that information to you. It could be a short survey or a quick QA or a request for them to engage in the comments of a blog post, for example. If the feedback you get indicates that anything is wrong with the content, you can improve your content marketing strategy and build a better brand reputation based on the feedback you've received.

To get an in-depth analysis of aligning content with the brand, check out **"Branding and Marketing: Practical Step-by-Step Strategies on How to Build your Brand and Establish Brand Loyalty using Social Media Marketing to Gain More Customers and Boost your Business"** by searching for it on the store.

Your Quick Start Action Step:

Analyze your website copy, blog posts, and social media

posts to see what kind of effect they have on the readers. Does your content impact your brand mission properly? If not, it's time to make some amendments and get back on track.

Chapter 5:
Know Your
Targeting Audience

Chapter 5: Know Your Targeting Audience

5.1 What is Your Target Audience?

It is difficult to know just how to find your target market, but not impossible. I'm going to give you my three favorite ways to find and understand the target market of your business.

A target audience is a group of people or consumers that are specifically interested in your product. Your target audience can be anyone, ranging from a kid to an adult. Your audience can be of any age group or any gender. The most important thing is that your target group has needs, requirements, or desires that *you* can fulfill.

Many companies don't understand their target market. And that can make targeting a significant challenge. However, these companies are not the only businesses that struggle with targeting. What about companies that are just starting and have an idea of who their market is, but have yet to really narrow down that audience? And what about companies that want to expand into different markets? What about clients who have never even given it a single thought? Dive into the details. Is he a man, is she a female, how old are they? What does their household look like? What is their lifestyle? Are they wealthy? Are they middle class? Find the audience's demographic and cater to it. Dive in as deep as you can, exploring as many different examples as possible. One of the other ways that you can explore your target demographic is if your business has a track record of people engaging via their social media. If you have people liking or commenting on your content or your customers leaving reviews, utilize that information. Learn everything you can about that person. Where do they live, what do they care about, what does their family look like? And yes, I know this is kind of terrifying. I promise you wouldn't be a stalker; you're just a marketer. What I highly recommend, though, is diving in as far as you can, find out what else they like and what their interests are. This is going to give you a great insight into your business's target market. If you can hop into the audience insights, learn absolutely everything that you can. Where do they live, what languages do they speak, what is their average income? How many kids do they have, what kind of car do they drive? Those types of insights are invaluable and can transform the way you're going to market as a social media manager.

5.2 Importance of Knowing Your Target Audience

Learning your target audience is one of the first steps you need to take when marketing any business. Many people think that their target audience is everyone interested in their business or service. But that's wrong, that is way too general. Instead, you need to narrow down everyone into a small group of people who both want and have means to buy your product or service.

There are a variety of factors that highlight the importance of knowing the target audience:

1. You know which area to target - For example, if a consumer lives in an area that is inaccessible based on your shipping budget, you shouldn't ship your products to them. If the consumer doesn't have the means to buy a product or service, this consumer is *not* a part of your target audience. You can't market high-end luxury cars to people who could never afford them, even if they

saved for a lifetime.

2. Save your money on marketing - When you focus just on the market which is more likely to buy your products, you spend the money wisely. This approach is more effective than just shooting in the dark and hoping for a sale or two.

3. You get an idea of the type of audience you have - Some people mix up two terms - "target audience" and "target market," but actually, there is a bit of difference between these two terms. The target market is everyone interested in your product or service. The target audience is a group of people *within* your target market to whom you direct your specific marketing campaign. For instance, let's say you need to buy a car you go to the car dealership. The salesperson without asking you any questions start showing you two-seater convertible sports cars because he thinks that you are a sporty woman who seems adventurous and this car will suit you better. But in reality, you are a mom of two, and you are looking for a big family car, so this salesperson loses his sale because he doesn't have any information about you and is just offering you the top-price product that *he* would like to own.

4. You have plenty of methods to the target audience - If you have an existing database, you should review the data it to see what these people have in common. Their interests and characteristics can be analyzed because most probably know other people who are similar to them who will be interested in buying your product as well.

5. You connect with your audience personally - Interact with your audience, talk to them, open the conversation, ask questions, create surveys around live streams. All of these things will help you to get in with your audience and will help you gain an understanding of what they need and what they are looking for.

6. Your competitors can pave your path - Check out the competitors and see what they are doing. Maybe there is an issue that they are overlooking so you can start targeting within that niche. It's essential to do the research all the time and see what other people are doing--what's working for them, and what isn't. Use this research to guide you as you narrow down your target audience.

7. Know your audience at a deeper level - You need to choose a specific demographic to target like age, family,

marital status, gender, income level, education, occupation, etc. You also need to consider the personal characteristics of the person, including values, interests, lifestyle, behaviors, and more. Find out when and how a target audience reaches your product, what features are the most appealing to them, what media they use to search for a piece of information: is it online, or maybe they attend particular events?

Once you answer all these questions, you need to summarize everything you have learned. Are there enough people who fit your criteria? Are they interested in your product or service? Do they have the means to buy your product or service? How easily can you find them and reach them with your message? Once you get to know the importance of your target audience, you'll know where to find your customer base. Then it's easier to find out what makes them buy your product or service. You shouldn't try to appease every single person who expresses a passing interest in your product; you need to target only that specific group of people who will buy your product or service.

5.3 How to Find Your Target Audience

How do you reach your target audience? Let's take a

look at some examples. Let's take a jewelry owner who wants to reach her audience on Instagram, and it's a particular audience of African-American women who buy jewelry. How can she reach them? Well, the goal is not to get in front of everybody on Instagram, but to get in front of the women who are most likely to buy.

It's not enough to be on the right social media network, because although Facebook has 1.5 billion users and may seem like the ideal platform, other networks are getting more and more users every day. You want to ensure that you're not just getting in front of the right people, but that you're getting their attention--and that all starts with knowing your audience. If you're just starting a business, you may not be entirely sure of this yet, but the best way for you to identify your target audience is to consider your social media strategy. Even if you are an advanced marketer, I still recommend that you take the time to give this some thought because it allows you to truly fine-tune who your customers are and where they are at on social media. This is the first step to getting to know and reach your audience, and you're going to accomplish that through using an effective social media strategy.

There are four main ways that you can reach your target audience online:

1. The first way to reach your target audience is through content. Once you know who your target audience is, you'll know what types of content they're interested in. So, as with our previous example, if you are trying to reach African-American women who want to buy jewelry, the content that you show them is going be very different than the content you would show someone who likes to look at different jewelry designs or who wants to learn how to make their jewelry. You'll have to gain a definite idea of what content will appeal to your most profitable target audience.

2. Then you can start using hashtags that help customers who are looking for something online and conducting searches to find what they're looking for on social media. And social media platforms like Facebook and Instagram dig deeper through hashtags. Thus it's a great strategy to get in front of the audience. A solid hashtag can get your product or service on the screens of those who are looking for what you have to offer.

3. You can also use social media tagging to mention people and brands in your content, and they will be

notified that they've been mentioned. Direct tagging can also boost your customer engagement and visitors.

4. Lastly, you can always advertise on online directories like Yelp or YellowPages. A lot of customers search for specific businesses online, and these websites can help boost your perceived reliability. Now, all of these previously mentioned strategies are free and organic ways of reaching your audience, but advertising is a way that you will be *guaranteed* to reach your audience. So if you try other methods and they're working, but not quite as quickly as you would like them to, then you can do advertising.

Your Quick Start Action Step:

Dive into your social media pages and check to see whether your posts are creating enough boom about your brand. Revise your previous content marketing strategy if you are not targeting your ideal audience or customers.

Chapter 6: Writing and Posting Content that Sells

Chapter 6: Writing and Posting Content that Sells

6.1 Attracting Customers through Content

Shareable Content

Do you know the recipe for delightful content that gets shared as soon as it gets posted? This type of content is called *shareable content.* A piece of shareable content compels the customers to happily and willingly share that content. According to research, a news story or a post that has a positive impact gets shared quickly. Any piece of content that creates a sense of excitement, happiness, frustration, or even anxiety gets more shares than any bland or boring content. What do you learn from this? You should only create the type of content that tends to make people react.

Another aspect of shareable content is having visual appeal. If your content focuses on quality over quantity, then kudos to you! It's always delightful to see limited content that attracts eyes rather than chunks of irrelevant content. So to create such content, you can try subheadings, bullets, and opt for small fonts.

When you have a well-established shareable content, then you can eventually attract people with similar interests. The more people who share your content, the more they attract other users to your post. Your content must be relatable to the current circumstances of your customers to be shared by them.

Customer Experience

Your customers can often become your brand advocates if they have an amazing experience at your website. *Customer experience* can be defined as "every experience, feeling, or action your customer has at your website." Are your customers clicking on a particular page? Are they bouncing back again and again from your website? What makes them leave your website? Are they happy with your social media posts? All of these things explain what exactly your customer experience is. So this is something you shouldn't avoid. You must know how vital it is to be a customer-centric business. And a customer-centric company needs to have its content created according to its customer's experience. Content marketing helps create a better customer experience.

When your content is created with the customer

experience in mind, then it creates a unique image of your brand in the industry. Your customers can trust you more, and they prefer to visit you again and again. And guess what? It can even increase your ROI.

Thus, a best practice to provide the ultimate customer experience is to create accurate content. A content that is concise, to-the-point, and has stunning visual appeal is something you can count on.

Attracting Customers through Content

Are you struggling with your content marketing methods and not sure where exactly to go from where you stand? You know about the internet. You know the number of people using it. But the most challenging part is to understand how to get to those potential customers who are actually willing to spend money on your product or service.

You need to know about the four methods you can use to attract new consumers with your impeccable content marketing:

• The first thing to do is create content on major blogs and media websites to get the attention of the new customers. For example, a website such as Forbes.com.

- Second, create a compelling lead-magnet offer.

- Third, create a high-conversion lead-capture webpage.

- Fourth, craft an automated email follow-up campaign.

Step 1 is the beginning of your journey. Here, you build a custom lead-capture webpage. This will help convert the right prospects into sales with compelling messaging that addresses your ideal target customer's wants and needs.

Step 2 is where you create a persuasive lead-magnet offer. This lead magnet should be apt enough to describe a customer's need and how you can solve that problem or otherwise address that need with a desirable result within a specific time frame. For example: "Learn to do digital marketing and enhance your skills in 1 week." When you post this lead magnet, what will you get in exchange for your trouble? Your customer's phone numbers and email addresses. This lead magnet must be able to solve your ideal customer's problem, and it can be in any format like a document, PDF, survey, discount, whitepaper, or a spreadsheet.

The visitor will click to receive that lead magnet, and they will do this in exchange for the coveted valuable information that you are providing to them. This information creates a funnel of ideal and interested customers. This method can give you a series of potential prospects that are having a problem willing to trust *you* to help them solve.

Step 3 is where you attract the customers further by engaging in frequent follow-ups. This is what we call "re-engaging." Your emails should provide information that encourages prospects to call, click, visit, or make an appointment. Through these follow-up emails, further value is provided and helps encourage the customer to get engaged in the upcoming steps in the buying process.

The last and final step of getting new customers over to your product is when your prospects click on a call to action. The previous process creates a sense of confidence in your customers, and that compels them to take action so that they become a part of your buying journey. This series of steps serves to convert a lot of prospects into recurring customers. The process mentioned above is necessary to keep your prospects connected to your content by giving them an offer that benefits *them*. Follow these steps and watch your conversion rate soar.

6.2 Why Customer Experience is Important

Seventy percent of web searching is owned by Google, whether it is a keyword search or images or maps. And there is a specific team appointed to check what their customer's experience is because searches are not evolving--customer behaviors are evolving. They are learning the algorithm and how to put it to use for them. The most critical element is what is happening to user behavior or customer behavior. When we are on mobile, we don't want to wait for crazy pop-ups, and we refuse to wait too long on a download from a slow website.

We don't ever have to chase an algorithm if we pursue our customers. Take your customer's problems and consider them as if you are the one facing those issues. When you get a feel of how your customers feel when they are visiting your blog, website, or social media post, it makes it easier for you to envision their experience and put that vision to work for you. Align your goals to your customer's goals. If you can't get new customers, you can genuinely focus on retaining the customers you already have. And the critical factor to this is focusing on customer experience. It's not about services or products--it's about how you are solving your customer's problems. It's also about brand protection. A challenge to face is that there is so much information to consider. There are so many channels, there are so many places there are so many tactics, and how does all of that align to your goals? The most important thing is identifying your target. Once your goal is defined, you then have to consider which channels and tactics you're going to use to accomplish those goals, and how you will plan across the customer journey.

What are you going to do? Picture this: If you're traveling by plane and you are lost in thought and only grab one of your bags from the bag return--but you brought two--wouldn't it be great if an airline employee flagged you down and said, "Hey, this is your bag!"? Of course! That is the type of scenario you want to create with your customers. Your goals, tactics, and channels--all of these are arranged based on the customer journey.

If you have many visitors but not a lot of customers, then you've got a severe issue. Your biggest concern then is going to be what's happening at your website. Another case to consider is where you're getting a lot of conversions, but most of the people converted are not even coming to the website--because the information is taken from your site and going onto a different website. People on top of your conversion funnel are probably not going to come to the site; they're going to different places. What do you need to do here? Make sure that you align everything based on your ultimate goal. So, if your goal is to gain new customers, and it's not a necessity to focus on conversion, your tactic has to be about doing a branded search. If your goal is to protect your customer, then your tactic has to be securing your brand. Different tactics will be employed based on your goals, what you want to accomplish, and based on where you are in your customer journey.

All of these things can be done if you do your work while keeping your customer experience in mind. Your product or service can hit the market, but it is the customers who decide whether your services are any good or not.

Think about your customers: What do they want, what do you know about them, and how can you create a valuable and personalized experience for them? The answers to these questions evolve from gaining an understanding of user intent. Our customers' intent is something we need to figure out for ourselves based on the information made available to us because unlike the brick-and-mortar store world where we could see these customers face-to-face, these customers are all online.

You have many means available for converting a customer, from the discovery phase to the buying phase and the post-experience phase. This is universal and applies to every business out there. Discovery starts with when the customers are thinking about something, and then they begin thinking about engaging with the vendor. When they are thinking about looking for a vendor and planning, that's when you know they're serious about that product. In many instances, they are thinking about hundreds and hundreds of ideas, but they stop their research when they reach a particular product or brand. Why does this happen? It's all due to past experience, or the experience of your current customers. Buying is that final transaction, and post-experience comes in after all these three phases are completed. Post-experience matters more than you might think because this is the phase where you can build that trust in your customer and create a sense of rapport between your business and the customer. In the digital world, you can learn about your customers through data. You can learn all about the customer and check who is visiting your website, what they want, what needs they have, and how your business might meet those needs. There are a lot of attributes that you want to know before you start creating strategies for your customers.

Let's say you're thinking about taking a vacation. You are looking through everything related to your vacation experience, like what there is to do at your destination, how the hospitality is at the restaurants and hotels in the area, what payment methods are available. You want to know what others are saying, so you read the reviews and narrow your options from there.

Search engines cannot index you if you don't have ripe information. Relevant information appropriately packed is what is fundamental for every business to help create the best customer experience. Nobody cares about you offering this product or having this beautiful brand. They're looking for how *you* are going to be able to help *them* or what kinds of things there are to do. People are looking less at the brand itself; they don't necessarily care if someone else is in love with your brand--they are going to come to your site if you treat *them* right.

6.3 Steps to Engage Customers by Providing Ultimate Experience

There are six steps to create the ultimate experience for the customers through content:

1. Research your audience and your competition - Start by having a solid content marketing strategy. Collect data about their demographic, such as income, age, area, gender, and more.

2. After learning about your audience, you need to create a format for your content posts. You should consider creating blog posts, as this is the most familiar and useful form of content marketing. Other than blog posts, add additional content like reports, podcasts, webinars, case studies, eBooks, slideshows, whitepapers, and videos.

3. Create content in accordance with the buyer's journey. Don't hesitate to create content that goes along with every aspect of your business or product. This helps the buyers solve their problems at every turn.

4. Apart from creating content, it's also important to *manage* content at every step. Create content according to the topics and sort these topics on your website according to their relevance.

5. Another tip is to optimize your website. How can you engage customers if they cannot navigate through the site with ease? To do this, you should add a comment section to every post, suggest inbound links to them, allow social media sharing, and add a call to action to attract them.

Your Quick Start Action Step:

To make your content marketing strategy profitable, you should plan your content according to your goal. Make sure you create content that aligns with your business goals. This ensures brand recognition and marketing benefits together in one stroke. The content should be shareable at every post and page. Consider integrating social media sharing on your website.

Create content that is visually attractive so your viewers can share your content as soon as they visit you. Adding that share button to your content is the key to increasing the number of shares your content gets.

Leave a Review:

As an independent author with a small marketing budget, reviews are my livelihood on this platform. If you enjoyed this book, I'd really appreciate it if you leave your honest feedback. I love hearing from my readers and I personally read every single review. You can do so by visiting this book's product page.

Chapter 7: Content Marketing Strategies

Chapter 7: Content Marketing Strategies

7.1 Content Marketing Strategy

For both the successful business as well for the new business, the content marketing strategy is crucial. When you plan, create, and post your content on different online platforms, that content marketing is called strategic content marketing. The process of taking the content and using a strategic plan so that it eventually leads to a sale is called a content marketing strategy. This strategy is evaluated at every platform, including blogs, social media, websites, and more. Why do you need a solid content marketing strategy? The answer is to build a business reputation and to achieve business goals.

As marketing costs and ad costs to use platforms such as Google, Facebook Marketing or even Instagram continue to go up, approaches like content marketing and SEO become ever more important because it doesn't cost any money after that piece of content has been created--it just keeps going forever and ever.

Content marketing is utilizing any type of content, whether that be something physical or digital, and turning it into a valuable, informational or entertaining asset, or a combination of all of the above: infotainment. You take your content and turn it into something that your potential audience will use and find practical. This way, they can decide what the content offers them and use it in their day-to-day lives, and it provides value to their day.

Characteristics of a Perfect Content Marketing Strategy:

- Identify your best platforms. Where are your customers spending their time online? Are they on Facebook, are they on Instagram? Are they looking at Medium, are they on YouTube, are they coming to your blog? Think about that and identify the best platforms for reaching your audience. Your business may be better suited to marketing content on some platforms than others, and that is perfectly okay. Narrow your focus to the platforms where your customers are. Give some thought to which platforms are best targeted when it comes to the product or service you offer and get yourself on there, ready to connect with customers.

- Build your content library. Do a lot of research and collect content upfront. There are a variety of different ways to do that, and a variety of different types of content. Give some thought to the different types of content. Let's take a few examples. One type of content is customer reviews. You can capture all these customer reviews and build out a stockpile of this type of content that you can trickle out on social media over time, or on all your different content sources and platforms. Another example would be infographics or stats. Do you have specific infographics or stats for your industry? These don't need to be graphics and statistics that you've created yourself; these could be the stats and infographics generated by other sources but *are related to your business.* You can collect a big library of these statistics or infographics that would be interesting and valuable to your followers to see (make sure you cite those sources!). You can then later use that data to create some of your own design assets. Some other examples would be finding quotes--industry-specific quotes or quotes that you have come up with yourself--and build out an inventory for those. Videos are a type of content, as are images--photos of your company, pictures of your products. If you build out this idea library, adding on all these different content types and really stockpiling these out in advance, you will save a ton of time moving forward when you need content "in the now" to post under your social media platforms.

- Create your cadence. What are you posting, what types of content are you providing to your audience every day? Or every week? When you are building your content library, you'll have all these different ideas and all these different types of content that you want to provide. Once you do that, you'll be able to visualize what you want to post. So you may wish to post a quote in the morning, and then post a stat in the afternoon, and possibly post a video in the evening. This is just an example. But you need to have a cadence, so there's something of a rhythm to your social media posts. Whether it's a daily rhythm or a weekly rhythm, you have that cadence--that thought that you've put into it in advance so that you know what type of content you need for the week or for the day. If you have your idea library, it is going to make it much easier to fall into this cadence than if you were just trying to post useful content off the top of your head. As opposed to thinking about that at that very moment. So give some thought to what type of cadence would be appropriate for your business and what would drive value to your viewers.

- Develop a posting schedule. Once you have your content library built up and you've considered the type of cadence that would be appropriate for your business and provide value to your customers, you need a regular schedule for making your content marketing strategy into a tangible reality. What does your schedule look like? Will you be posting one time a day, three times a day, five times a day? Under which platforms will you be posting content? Do you need to post multiple content types to various platforms? We would recommend posting between one and three times a day on each platform you decide to use for your content marketing. The three times per day approach is beneficial to you because you could be reaching your audience when they wake up, when they eat lunch, and when they go to bed. Studies show that this is when people look at content most often. If you schedule three types of content to post during those particular times of the day, that will be perfect. And then figure out the cadence: Are you posting quotes in the morning, videos in the afternoon, that kind of thing? Once you've made that happen, it will be time to develop your schedule template. When you do this, think in terms of building a schedule template for the week, that way you can use your template each week as a guide, and you can populate the template with the content for your posts during the week.

- Document as you go. The idea library is fantastic for just pre-populating all this content so you hardly even have to think about it. When you add in the cadence and the schedule, you have posts that are ready to go, scheduled and dialed in. But aside from that, you also need to document as you go. So as cool things happen, you come across things, you take pictures of stuff, you do some live videos of yourself, so document as you go, and that way you can post this stuff in real time as it occurs. You can layer that in on top of your pre-fabricated, pre-scheduled content. You can also look at what works, what causes click-throughs and engagement, and what doesn't. This way, you can document what content works and what may need to be reshaped or pulled altogether.

- Be efficient. Use a tool like Hootsuite, which is a tool that lets you pre-schedule your posts, so they send out at the correct times. It also contains some metrics in there that you can use from a results perspective, to get a better look at how you're doing. The system also allows you to do some engagement, which is nice because it will enable you to streamline a lot of these activities that would otherwise be done by hand, one by one, which can get time-consuming--and time is money. You can pre-schedule things to post to various social media platforms using one tool like Hootsuite to do all of this in one place.

- Engagement. You don't want to necessarily just be pushing content all the time. With social media marketing, in particular, you want to be *social,* so you want to like, comment, follow other people, and engage with the community. Be involved. So don't just post your content, actually be an active engager of *other* content. This is going to help you increase your brand awareness, and essentially grow your followers over time, and it will do so much more quickly than if you're exclusively pushing your own content.

- Add value. Don't just post for the sake of merely posting. Make sure that every post delivers some kind of value to your followers. Otherwise, they'll stop following you and stop engaging with you--and stop buying from you. Share-worthy content plus share-worthy design, plus engagement, equals success. And the key to all of that is delivering value, every time.

- Track your results, and make adjustments accordingly. If you see that you've gotten more engagement, more likes, more sharing, of your posts that are made in the evening, consider doing more posts in the evening, or adjust the times that your posts are going live. In another example, if you see a particular type of post that you're doing, maybe it's one where you're highlighting different stats in your industry, and you see that this one has a lot of engagement, consider doing some more of those and see if you continue to build more engagement when you do. If another post, like your customer reviews, isn't doing as well, consider doing fewer of those. So, look at your data, start to understand what your followers want to see, and give them more of what they like. It's common sense, but it's also effective marketing.

- Find some social media role models. Find some role models in your industry, who you think are doing a great job on social media, who are delivering content value to you. Then, you can do a bit of reverse engineering, and give some thought to how you can use some of those ideas as inspiration for yourself. This can help guide you in the type of content and strategy that you can successfully implement for *your* brand.

- Stay relevant. Make sure that you're relevant to

the subject matter for your social media content and your brand. People who are following you for advice and information on, say, quality dance clothes, don't really care what you did this weekend when you went kayaking or in seeing pictures of your dog; they're not so interested in that. What they *are* interested in, though, is dance apparel. If that's your niche and your industry, stay within that wheelhouse. Talk about that, be an expert on that, add value to that, and *that* will be what increases your following.

- Brand your social media platforms. Make sure they're professionally designed, streamlined and consistent, that you have good profile pictures, and that you populate all the areas of content. The about us, your website links, your other social links, videos, don't ignore a single populated field. Because what's going to happen is people who are following you, and like your content, at some point, they're going to want to move forward with your brand.--possibly to become a customer. When that happens, you want them to be able to do that right from your social platform, very quickly. You want to be accessible so that people will be able to click through to your website, see your call to action, and take that next step. By taking the time to brand those social media platforms, you have that laid in so that it's a smooth conversion funnel for your followers.

- Invest in a paid advertisement. Although providing content and engaging with followers (and following relevant others) are compelling from an organic perspective, paid advertisement can take things to the next level and get you some serious sales boosts. Doing some campaigns, spending some money boosting your post, gets it out in front of more people than you would be able to do organically alone. Do some retargeting campaigns, and some other things on the paid side, to supercharge your growth on the social side.

- Don't stop doing it. Keep focusing on your content strategy. So many times we see good content start coming out from a brand, and then it stops. Poof. What that means is the content provider just stopped investing time in it. They stopped putting manpower behind it. You need to make sure you stay consistent. You're not going see tremendous growth overnight. But if you continually post content and keep an eye on your content strategy and engage with your followers, you're going to go from 100 followers to 1,000 eventually after several months, to 2,000, and three years from now it could be hundreds of thousands. The question is: Did you stick with it or not? Because the growth is there, it's just something you need to keep working on and continue optimizing. So if you do not have time to invest in it yourself, hire somebody, or hire another company to do it for you, but just make sure that you're investing in doing it to get results.

How a content marketing strategy works:

1. The first step to do is to create your goals and objectives. Content flow planning is just any kind of planning involved in the creation and implementation of your content. I find it is useful because it allows you to be able to draw arrows to things and line things up in a diagram. Goals and objectives should be

considered: Are you trying to drive leads with your content, are you trying to you know build sales for your content, are you just trying to inform your audience with your content?

2. Digital marketing agencies can help to target specific keywords. If you want to start ranking higher, you need to get the content that you want to rank at number one on Google or YouTube, and it's just up to what stage you're at in the funnel. Create a high-level strategy using specific keywords when creating content. Searching keywords for content marketing is like creating a sub-strategy. This sub-strategy focuses on main sets of keywords and gives you an idea of how to move forward with content creation.

3. Next, create your buyer personas. And if you don't have an idea who your buyer personas are, you can do some research to figure them out. These are the same people who are going to be engaging with your content. Review your objectives and think of demographics. For example, males between the ages of 18 to 35 who are entrepreneurs. If you spread this out a little bit so you get little room for entrepreneurs would be for marketers, college dropouts, or people never went to

college, people who want total personal control over their careers. Whatever characteristics your buyers have--that's what you want to lay out, because this helps you determine what you need to focus on to get this type of content to that person.

4. Another step you need to take is to get your content audited. The content audit is an in-depth analysis where you can see all keywords and their rankings. The content audit enables you to put all of this information together to figure out the best way to reach customers. To do this, you can use a tool called Google Search Console, and it shows you all of the traffic that your content receives. It's able to show you all of your keywords and their specific rank on the Google search engine. The only way you can do a content audit is if you have content currently, so if you are just beginning your content marketing journey, you can't perform a content audit yet. However, even new businesses have the option of analyzing your *competitor's* content. Look at the content of the competition. See how people engage and react to that kind of content.

5. Having a content management system can save you from a future headache. You can create, schedule, and

post your content directly from a content management system. There are many reliable CMS in the market, like WordPress, HubSpot, Hootsuite, and more.

6. After the content audit, you know where you stand currently and what keywords might be good for targeting. The next thing to do is get into the keyword research phase. Keyword research can be done with several tools like Google Keyword Planner--keywords everywhere. Another great tool is Ubersuggest. You'll start with your high-level keywords: for example, "marketing agency." This will give you a bunch of suggestions that can be used. In Google Keyword Planner, you go to the planner and click find "new keywords." To do this, you do have to have an ad manager account. Make sure you have that set up first, and then you can click to get started. Then it's going to start showing you the keywords as well as the competition. You need to opt to target lower competition with high search volume keywords. Then you'll need to create an Excel spreadsheet to keep a record of these keywords. It shows the keyword list, and their volume and the competition for that particular keyword. Next up is Google Trends. If you know your keywords but you're stumped on what to

choose first then this tool can be your guide. This tells how relevant a keyword is over time. It shows the searches according to their geographical area, allowing you to choose the best-trending keywords from your list.

7. The next step in content marketing is to prioritize the content. After collecting the keywords to create content, you can create a plan to use specific keywords for a specific time. The easier to target will be used first and then the rest. You can also create a schedule to publish content on a month-to-month basis. So prioritize your topics make sure that everything makes sense. You need to pick a niche in the beginning and stick with that niche and become the expert.

8. Finally, you need to set your content calendar. Once you prioritize your topics and your keywords, then you need to create article topics based on those keywords. Creating content off-the-cuff is not a great strategy, but creating consistent and engaging content is the most promising way to attract customers. On the other hand, a content calendar also reduces the load of content creation as well as it can help you in A/B testing. It's just making sure that you're doing everything and

planning everything to be well-executed. If you're not taking these steps, it's going to be difficult to create a content marketing plan that achieves success. Once you have the content marketing plan in place for the first 30 to 45 days, you can create a campaign-planning calendar, where you can go in and add topics for the future.

7.2 Why Content Marketing Strategy Is Important

Why is content marketing strategy so important for your business?

The following are some points that show the importance of content marketing strategy:

• You are probably already aware of how important it is to follow up with a person you have personally approached to convert them from a lead to a paying customer. Using pushy sales tactics and badgering with weekly follow-ups could lead to pushing them away rather than converting them. However, what if you deliver content to them that helped to educate them on the services or products you offer that interest them?

• By effectively utilizing content marketing strategy,

you start adding value, and you build trust. This is going to make you stand out from your competition and have a positive impact on your conversion rate because you will get more organic visitors to your website.

- Content marketing strategy gives you free and organic traffic you don't have to pay for. You do pay for the content that you put up on your website (blogs, videos, etc.) upfront. But once you start ranking for that content, if somebody sees your listing in the SERPs and they click on that organic result, then you're not paying for that traffic. This adds huge value to your website and will start generating new leads and sales 24/7.

- A solid strategy will help you to address buyer objections. By surveying your customers and prospects, you will conclude what their objections or needs are. Once you understand these things, then you should create content centered around that. You can then use that in your email follow-ups, blog posts, videos, and even in eBooks. Anything that can answer those buyer objections will help increase your conversion rates.

- You can use concepts for lead generation. For example, any paid ads that you're running, you can use those as free give away. To create a mini-eBook or a whitepaper or a checklist, something of value that helps educate your customers on whatever you do. That's a freebie, but it doesn't have to be a loss. You can give this content away for free, and the customer provides their name and their email address to you, which gives you a potential customer email list, and you can start dripping them with content.

- Creating a content strategy helps you get a series of new and recurring visitors, which you would not have otherwise had access to. By creating a content marketing strategy, you can convert leads to customers.

- A perfect content marketing strategy helps you to retarget your customers. For example, when somebody visits your site but doesn't contact you, so you don't have their email, and you don't know their information, but you did pixel them. Through looking at the tracking pixel, you will know which product they're interested in. This can help you retarget them with ads, and those ads can provide answers to those buyer objections.

They might have to click to that ad which could be a free download of some sort of content. This will get them to your email list and then convert them from a lead to a customer. Thus, a perfect content marketing strategy is the key to your business goals, whether it is being carried out via a website or on social media.

Another importance of content marketing strategy is to be used it along with the sales funnel.

Sales Funnels Strategy

You can create a content marketing plan from scratch. There are many reasons why you want to do this. Obviously, if you have some goals for your business, you need to achieve those goals. You need to follow a step-by-step process to be able to create a good content marketing plan.

Let's take an in-depth look at the sales funnel.

You have to understand what a sales funnel is in order to create a content marketing strategy. By default, funnels look a little bit different based on the individual business and a lot of people size them up in different ways, but generally, most people look at this the same way. There's a top of the funnel, middle funnel, bottom funnel, and the retention piece of the funnel.

The top part of the funnel is called the awareness, the middle is called consideration, the bottom is called conversion, and the tail-end of the funnel has the remaining customers after the sales, and is called retention.

The funnel operates from top to bottom, and you have to monitor and optimize it along the way.

At the top of this funnel is the very high-level stuff that you do to grab traffic initially. The main goals of the top part of funnel can be things such as increasing traffic, moving the customers to the next level of the funnel, and decreasing bounce rate.

The metrics that you need to keep in check to achieve your goals are clicks, bounce rate, time being spent on the site, and pages per session.

The middle funnel goals and metrics are different from those of the top funnel. This level's goals are things like lead generation, email list growth, tripwire sales, or low-dollar product sales. The metrics of this funnel could be the opt-in percentage, the tripwire conversion percentage, or the total absolute number of leads that are being generated for your business.

The next part of the sales funnel is the bottom funnel. The goals of this funnel can be conversions, or maybe lowering your cart abandonment rate. Metrics might be the average order value, revenue per visit, number of SKUs sold, or perhaps your abandon cart percentage rate are the metrics to track there. And finally, monetization, retention, and love.

After you've converted users, what you have to do with them? Well, the goals with these can be to create repeat buyers, to grow the value for those users for a lifetime, maybe reducing churn, or whether they could get some of their friends into your service or product. There are many metrics that you need to monitor for this funnel; or example, retention reports, customer lifetime value, or maybe net promoter score, fundamentally how happy your customers are.

This is the way you can optimize each part of the funnel and what the goals are for each stage of that funnel. You can make a template for a sales funnel and content marketing plan. List all the possible ideas that we have for content marketing. First, launch dynamic product ads on Facebook. Let's say you're an e-commerce company and you haven't done any ads on Facebook yet. You know how significant it is to attract customers through Facebook. For an e-commerce company, the bottom part of the funnel probably makes the most sense. Let's say you just hired and paid a lot of money for these amazing Facebook ads.

Next, you can write Twitter posts, as you know, this is great social media marketing. After that, you can create and upgrade the content on the blog, and give people our marketing guide (or another freebie applicable to your business) in exchange for an email address. At this stage, the middle funnel will be the area of impact.

Getting a few more email addresses, how impactful to the business would that be? It may not have as much impact as Facebook ads do so you might realize that upgrading the content on the blog is of lower priority than creating dynamic ads on Facebook.

The next step of the content marketing plan with regards to the sales funnel is to advertise on industry podcasts and build awareness. But what if you have a difficult time getting podcasters to feature your ads? This approach would then be less impactful, and you may have better results focusing your efforts on the content types and platforms that offer you and your business to create a more significant impact.

To carry out an analysis of the impact at each stage of the sales funnel, you can create a template. You can list it on the area of impact, such as at the top, middle, or bottom of the funnel, and then rate the impact and ease of a given content type or platform and it'll create an easy product roadmap for you.

7.3 Content Marketing Strategies for Various Platforms

Six things to keep in mind for a successful content strategy:

• When you set up a content marketing strategy, you create content for your targeted audience, and that audience consists of your readers or viewers. If you want to attract more customers to your content, you should set up a dedicated content marketing strategy for different platforms. As you know, each platform operates differently.

• The content marketing strategy works on the purpose of solving a specific problem of a particular group of people. On the other hand, your content should also be engaging enough, and it must educate or entertain the people viewing it. Thus, your content is a solution that compels your viewers to do business with you.

• Your content also sets you apart from your competitors, so make sure you set up a sophisticated content marketing strategy. You have to show what makes you different from the other fish in the sea, and you can prove that by providing amazing content.

• Consider the most effective format for your content. Is your content best suited to a blog? Video media? Podcasts?

• You need to figure out the channels where your content will be posted. It could be a website, or it could be a social media profile like Twitter or Facebook.

• The most important thing to note when setting up a content marketing strategy is to manage the content. Content marketing without management is like sailing without a boat. So, create a manageable content calendar, Excel files, and documents where your content will be adequately managed.

How to design a content marketing strategy for different platforms:

1. Blogs - Blog posts are an integral part of the website's content. Thus, ignoring blogs entirely or publishing blogs rarely are huge mistakes. You should write frequent and well-researched blog posts. These blogs can help deliver value to your brand. The ideal length of the blog post is between 1000 to 2000 words. Make sure that your blogs are shareable to different mediums. This way, when your users visit you, they gain a valuable piece of information, and they can share the information with others.

2. Ebooks - Ebooks are lengthened versions of blog posts. When users visit a blog post, but they want to know more about that topic, you can gracefully guide them to your eBook. The business that follows eBook distribution for their content marketing strategy is regarded as more professional than the one that does not. Ebooks can be placed at a landing page after blog posts alongside a call to action.

3. Case studies - Case studies act as opportunities to tell others about your customer's story. A case study can create an impact on the other visitors to your website. Case studies can take any form like a podcast, blog posts, or eBooks. The case study provides proof that

your product or service is the best that builds customer trust.

4. Templates - Templates are an excellent way to offer an insight into your service or product. They also act as a time-saving tool for your customers.

5. Infographics- Content like infographics are appealing to customers. You can easily share a lot of information on a single page, so create a clear infographic to share valuable data with your customers.

6. Videos - When nothing else works, videos can be the best content marketing strategy. When your customers see you speaking about your services, they tend to be more inclined towards using those services. Videos are highly shared content on social media platforms, so this is a great way to reach your customers through videos.

7. Podcasts - This is the most appreciated content form in recent years. The number of customers who prefer to listen to podcasts is increasing. You can interview a set of influential people and publish a podcast on your website or social media.

8. Social media - You have to become good at crafting content before you can do paid advertising. If you know how to do content marketing and you can engage with your current following, you can get an idea of what they're thinking. Now you have a better understanding of how people think and how they respond to you. Start out posting on your regular Facebook profile, Instagram profile and start posting YouTube videos. After this, you will start getting organic traffic because that's what happens with content marketing, as long as you stay consistent. You have to remain consistent with your content, and the more you do that, the more people are going to see your videos, images, or posts. Post on your social media profiles about your current content marketing strategy and look at the responses being given. From there, you will start understanding people better through their responses.

9. Website - The biggest challenge isn't creating the content; it's regularly producing new topics. So, if it appears like your time and mental energy are spent brainstorming ideas rather than actually creating the content itself, you're not alone. How to fix it? Try mapping out a list of topics to discuss in advance and scheduling their publishing dates and make a content

calendar. Plan ahead and see how your website and business flourish. Creating and promoting content is a necessity, yet finding the time to do it presents a real struggle for the busy entrepreneur. This is why it's so crucial to continually be on the lookout for fresh and better approaches to get your message out quickly and efficiently--so you can produce content that connects and then bring your focus back to your business.

Your Quick Start Action Step:

After creating your content, you need to work on content management. Work **according** to your content calendar and start posting content on every medium you've decided to use. Many ideas can be used continuously, but some other approaches can be used on a more periodical basis. Content marketing is not a process; it's an art form.

Chapter 8:
Putting it All Together: How to Come Up with a Content Marketing Plan for Successful Campaigns

Chapter 8: Putting it All Together: How to Come Up with a Content Marketing Plan for Successful Campaigns

8.1 Content Marketing Plan

Content marketing can be fruitful when there is a solid content marketing plan. Every business can be successful in its effort in spreading content to the customers provided that they use proper planning. In such a competitive world, it's crucial to have an effective content marketing plan.

Every business has a purpose, and to achieve that purpose content marketing acts as a roadmap. Many companies fail at creating a content marketing plan that *works*. What's the result? Their customers start fading out. A simple yet effective content marketing plan consists of what the content is, where to share, when to share, and how to share that content. This planning keeps everyone in your company engaged in the content marketing process. This will help you become aligned with your goal.

8.2 Why a Content Marketing Plan Is Needed

Content marketing refers to creating emails, blog posts, newsletters, social media posts, whitepapers, infographics, and more. When you set up a business strategy, the need to create a content marketing strategy that helps to achieve business goals becomes obvious. Content is the staircase through which a buyer accomplishes their buyer journey.

Scheduling Content Marketing Plan

There are three keys to a successful result when it comes to your content marketing. The first key is consistency. You've probably heard this before, but content marketing is a marathon, not a sprint. Thus, it's essential that even if it's just one or two posts a week, it's something that you can commit to and continue to do over and over again for months or years to come. Make sure that you don't bore your audience because you want to keep your content fresh, so you should not post five times a week about the same topic. We need to stay focused on what our audience cares about, and this is important. This is why it is crucial to rotate your topics so you remain relevant and stake consistently--plus, it gives you more chances to be in front of people.

Posting content is going to be the most important part. I suggest posting at least three core pieces of content per week. If that seems too overwhelming for you and all you can do is post one per week, then one per week is better than none per week. You have to recognize that it's going to take you much longer than you'd like to get the results that you're looking for. If you're only going to post once per week, you can try a trick to keep the content day. For example, on Monday you can post a particular topic and Tuesday a different topic and so on. That way you make sure that you're creating pieces of content for each one of those days and you're rotating through your pillars and topics. So, if you plan to post five times per week, then go ahead and create five different components. This way, you're talking about something relevant to your audience, but it's a different pillar piece of content each day so you're evenly rotating through things and you're not just talking about one topic for five or six days in a row (and boring your audience to tears).

Once you've decided how many times per week you're

going to post, it's time to plan out your content; this is where keywords and titles come into play. I highly recommend that you plan out at least a month in advance, and you do all of your keyword research and all of your title research and title writing in one sitting. That way, during the month, while you're going through and creating your content, there's a lot less friction in terms of anxiety. You're going to be able to be very strategic with the different topics, and you'll be able to space out your content and see everything that you're doing in a month. And then you can just put your head in the sand and make content and then come up for air the end of the month.

When it's time to do your content calendar again, the next step is syndication. At this point, you know what your core medium is, what your content pillars are going to be, and you've organized your posting days of the week based on those content pillars. Syndication makes it easier for you to use single content types at various platforms. For example, videos can be posted to YouTube, Instagram, Facebook, and more. Then on LinkedIn, we can create a pulse post, and on Facebook, we post the thumbnail and the link every once in a while. This is just an example of how you can take one piece of content and chop it up into little pieces and spread it out to other platforms. Now, of course, it's vital that it makes sense to chop it up and spread it out to other platforms. So if you're doing the content writing, you could then have someone record the content and turn it into a podcast, or you can read through it and turn it into a podcast yourself. If you don't want to be featured in front of a camera, you can take that audio and put it on YouTube and put up some slides that have that be the entire video. Podcasts work successfully for quite a few businesses so you can create a lot of content off of all of the initial work you did on just one of your core pieces of content.

You'll need to then go through your content calendar again and decide on which days you'll post on those syndication platforms. This works well if you're looking at only posting three times per week on your main platform. Maybe you will want to look into posting on those off days that you have on some other platforms that aren't going to require as much work. After all, you're just sending what you already put together.

Content Calendar Template

If you can't focus on content strategy alone, then you

can create a content calendar from scratch, because it is such an important step in your content marketing strategy. This calendar gives you a sense of relief and your business a schedule for content posts for the upcoming months. If you're into content marketing, and you're producing a lot of content, it's essential to create a content calendar. When are you posting? What time do you post? Who's handling which responsibility? The bigger your brand is, the more essential it becomes to have a content calendar for your content marketing purposes.

So how do you create and manage your content calendar in an efficient manner?

Let's have an in-depth look at some of the high-level goals before get going. What's the goal here? The goal is to create an editorial calendar to manage your team's content marketing efforts. The ideal outcome has a pre-set editorial calendar that offers a guideline about what and when you need to post the content. The content calendar works irrespective of where you want to publish it. It is just an implementation of the titles and days and times in which the content is to be posted.

In other words, it's not going to be this, "Hey guys, what

are we posting on Facebook tomorrow? Did someone post on LinkedIn? What are we tweeting right now?" *Everything* is managed through this one centralized document. That's how this works. Prerequisite to this, you need to make sure that your customer avatar is defined. This is also called a buyer persona, a user avatar, or a customer journey. All of these refer to the same thing. You have to be sure that you have well-defined customer avatars before you do this. A customer avatar is an archetype of a particular customer that you have.

The next requirement is to have your keyword strategy in mind. If you haven't performed your keyword research until now, make sure you do this as soon as possible. It is essential to know the basic keywords before you can add them to the content calendar. There are a bunch of resources on keyword research like Google Keyword Planner and more.

Why is it essential to have a content marketing calendar? Having a content calendar secured helps your entire team save time, be on point, and figure out all the efforts they want to execute for a whole year. You can centralize all the things you need and more efficiently plan out the weeks, months, and years ahead. Set it and forget it. That's very powerful.

Whether you're on the SEO team, the email team, the social team or if you're a small team and there are two or three people doing everything, this is a great way to centralize your plan.

Where is this done? You are going to do this in Google Sheets as well as on Trello. Trello works as a web-based project management board so that you can use both of those. Trello.com is free to use, and the premium account for these tools costs around $5 a month. So go ahead and get an account there before you get started.

When is this done? You must have to do this any time you have decided to stop being so sporadic about your content marketing placement, and you have to centralize this and make it a repeatable, expected process throughout your content marketing efforts.

Who does this? It could be you. It could be the webmaster, or your content manager, or an agency that you've hired.

Get started making a content calendar and make a copy for yourself in your own Google Drive folder. One thing you may want to do before you get started is brainstorm. You can do this by setting up a meeting with your team members. Each member of your team can suggest a content idea that can be added into the calendar. These ideas must correspond to your customer avatars.

It is a representation of your customer's wants and needs and desires. Think of every conceivable content piece that can be useful to your customers and just put it into a Google Sheet. Don't prioritize it. Don't worry too much in the beginning. Add it, even if it is a rough idea. Be more liberal about this at the beginning and add more content as you can. You can then work at optimizing it and whittling it down a bit later. Let's say we were working at a company that was designed for New Jersey wedding venues, and we are hoping to get new customers who are willing to book weddings. We are trying to get couples that are looking for a place to book their wedding. We would need to brainstorm ideas for our content marketing calendar. So, have a brainstorm session in which you can come up with any concepts at all. Just give some thought to how your users would search for things and what your users may find helpful. So, the concepts could be the best millennial wedding venues, funniest wedding videos of 2019, best wedding invitation ideas. Whatever it is. You can sort of do this ad research for as long as you can. Just throw a bunch of ideas in there.

As you go along, if you decide to use them, you can schedule them so that you can make a note of that here. So, under "scheduled," answer yes or no. Which topic is "no" and which is "yes," adding the actual date you publish them. Once you've exhausted this, you have all your ideas in there. You can switch over to the actual template. So, publish date will be the date on which you will publish this content. We'll just pick a day in the future, and we will say June 15th, 2019.

The due date is usually one or two days before your actual publish date in order to fix spelling errors and have an editor look at it. So you'll have your due date two days prior to publication. The author has to be very self-explanatory. Let's say you really like this idea of wedding venues for millennials. This will be your keyword that you might want to change to an actual title.

You can opt for something like, "Best Wedding Venues For Millennials In 2019." The title is a brief explanation of what your actual content would be. You have got your primary keyword, then you would do some keyword research in this instance, and you come to know that the keyword "best wedding venues for millennials" have the most number of searches.

Then go to your target persona; usually, you've already created your buyer persona at this point. Let's say you have a buyer target persona named Sheena and Sheena is a 24- to-30-year old who's about to get married. And if you're familiar with the sales funnels, you must know there are always visitors at every part of the funnel, and usually at the top, middle or bottom funnel.

This type of content feels like it belongs at the top of the funnel. Therefore, the offer will probably be to get their email address in exchange for something. So maybe the offer here can be creating a checklist for the keyword wedding venues for millennials. And then the content type. Is it a blog post? Is it a video? Is it a social post? Is it a photo? Is it a digital tool? This will depend on your business and its needs.

In many instances, it will become the title of a blog post so that you can write a blog post title, and that's all there is to it.

That's just one example of how to create a content calendar template and lay out the entire process for yourself and have it all set it up for the whole year. With this template, you just brain dump all of your ideas, and then actually decide which ones you want to publish later on. That's the template to use to scale out the whole plan for the year--but managing the process is a little bit different. This is where Trello comes in. You can use a Trello board to manage that process. Merely creating an editorial calendar isn't enough.

In this way, you get a really clean, straightforward way to manage the content, as well. Once you are signed up with Trello, you can go to your content calendar and go into the Trello account. This tool is beneficial to manage your content calendar so that you can create relevant content for your customers.

The basic idea here is you can insert various ideas into your calendar and assign various topics to different members of your content management team. Once you're on the Trello board, you have to go to "Show Menu" and go to "More," and go ahead and click "Copy Of The Board."

Call it whatever you want, "Content Calendar Template

Sample 2019" or whatever you'd like, and you're good to go. You need to add every type of content that was created by you, and that you decided to create posts for. Here, you do not need to add brainstorm ideas, but the main keywords that are best to target buyer persona. You're going to add that to your "To Do" list and plug it directly into the Trello board.

Then we'll jump into the tool. So add the "Best Wedding Venues For Millennials" in there. Under the "To Do" list, you'll go to add a card, and you will add that here, where we can dump all of the other keywords into, as well. "Funniest Wedding Videos 2019" and "Best Wedding Invitation Ideas" can be added, along with different keywords that you are going to post later on. So you can add all of your cards there first in the "To Do" section.

Once you have all your ideas in there, you can go in and start assigning them. Make sure you get all your other team members on Trello too. You can go ahead and add members there and assign them different tasks within Trello.

You can also give them different labels. Your keyword can be your label, as well. Let's say you want this to be in long-form content, 5000 plus words. You'll make that green. Then you can create and add labels to these other keywords too. Suppose you want to add a video on "Funniest Wedding Video to 2019," so add a label on there.

You can also give its own color. So you can also label your content based on what kind of the type of content that it is. When you're in these cards, you can also add comments. So it's going to be a funny video. Thus, go ahead and add comments to the "funniest wedding videos of 2019"'s card. Whatever comment it requires, you can leave your comments there, as well. Trello also lets you add a due date, making it a handy tool when it comes to content calendar creation.

Creating a due date is simple. You can go in and make it whatever you'd like and hit "Save." Whenever staff or your team is working on something, you're going to want them to move that Trello card into the "Work In Progress" board.

If you are going to create this content for your designated keyword "Best Wedding Venues For Millennials," you can move this over to Work In Progress. Once you have finished that, you can tell your manager or someone else on the team is in charge of reviewing it. Then you move the card over to "In Review." So someone responsible for proofreading everything would review it, then hitting "Publish" in order to mark the item complete.

Once it's published, you'd move it over again into the "Published" board. If there's a snag, and something is wrong, and you want to scrap the idea entirely, you can move it over to "Not Doing." By following these steps and using the template you have already created and you use the Trello board template, it's going to make your life a lot easier, more organized, and hopefully it will help you to grow your business.

Queries before creating a content marketing plan:

So question number one is: What want or need does your product or business address? Understanding the paying point of your customers is vital when it comes to marketing, so thinking through what need or want you're filling is where it starts.

Question number two is: What's your target market? When you're thinking about this, think about the "who, what, when, where, and why" of your customers: Who are they, what state are they in, why are they in that state, where are they, is there a geo-location there, and where are they spending their time online? Do they watch videos on YouTube or Facebook or Instagram, do they search on Google? Truly understanding the demographics of your customers, from age to gender to interests, the things they do, the lifestyle that they live, understanding all these things is key to success.

Question number three is: Who are your competitors? And if you don't have direct competitors, think about other products or services that try to fill the void that *you're* trying to fill. When you know about your competitors, do a lot of research. Understand what they're doing, what they are doing for marketing, what does their presence looks like, what is on their website, what are their price points? Even consider calling them or buying their product so you can experience it firsthand.

When you have all this information, the key thing you're trying to find out here is what makes you *different*. You need differentiation in the marketplace, so understanding your competitors allows you to know what *you* do differently, even though you're selling the same thing or providing the same service. And there's a reason you do it differently: it's because you think that way is *better*, so understanding this makes you able to articulate that in your marketing.

Question number four is: What are the goals of your marketing campaign, both short term and long term? Begin with the long term. How many sales do you want to receive, or how many leads do you want to acquire within six months or a year, or two years? What does that look like, and what's your marketing budget to achieve that, what's your ultimate cost-per-acquisition goal? Try to understand all these end-goal metrics, after which you can reverse engineer them back into bite-size pieces and realistic expectations to ramp up. Because marketing doesn't work overnight, so you don't want to expect those returns initially, but you *do* want to come to expect them in the long term, so ask yourself how to get there. Reverse engineering that, and building achievable goals in the early months will give you that sense of confidence and the overall view that you need to drive success over the long term.

Question number five is: What is your strategy on the search and social? This is where people spend all their time today; either they are on a search engine looking for something, or they are doing social media engagement--so how will you reach them there? What types of keywords on a search do you need to rank for? That's inbound search; that's when people are at the hottest state of wanting to take action, so how do you rank high there so that you have the necessary visibility? Then you ask yourself, how do you get in front of people on social media? What social channels do your customers spend their time on, what type of content excites them, what would catch their eye, what type of campaign do you think would be engaging at that point to help them understand who your brand is and build that critical awareness? Really think through that strategy, because dominating search and social these days, when it comes to marketing, is the key to success.

Question number six is: What is your strategy for building a strong online reputation? Reviews are in trend today. This is where people look before they take action, before they buy a product or become a lead or buy a service, they're going to check your reputation online before getting in touch with you. Eighty-six percent of people do this kind of research before they ever even make a buying decision, so if you don't have a good reputation, you're losing a considerable amount of sales. What strategy can you apply here? What review sites you must be present on? It is ideal to be on multiple reviews sites, so learn which ones are relevant to your business, and then how to get reviews on those sites. What is your process for asking your customers for reviews? Is it a personal ask, an automated system of some kind that would be sending out automated emails and reminders? What is it you can do to make sure that you have a constant flow of new fresh reviews? If you have good reviews, and somebody's stuck with the decision of do I go with you or a competitor, they're going to choose you because *you* have the best reputation.

Question number seven is: What is your strategy to convert your leads into sales? Or if you're an e-commerce store, what's your plan to generate more sales per customer, to increase the revenue per customer? What's your sales strategy? What's your process there? If you have a great marketing campaign and you're creating all this activity, you're creating all this lead flow, all these online purchases, what are you doing to take full advantage of that, to turn those into additional sales, or turn them into sales at all? Think about that process, and then think about what sales collateral your sales team needs to do these things. What emails do you need to design, what infographics need to be created to demonstrate these things visually, what videos should you create to assist your team during the sales process, whether it's the new sales or the upsales, to help them achieve those goals and increase your ultimate return on investment?

Question number eight is: How do you build out automated journeys to leverage automation, to generate more sales and more activity with regards to email marketing and retargeting? What's going to happen if you're going to have people who take a look at your website or see your brand on social media? These things are automated to stay in front of those people and are a form of retargeting. You can retarget those people and stay in front of them. What do *those* campaigns look like? What do you retarget, what kind of message do you give them the first seven days after they go through your brand or go to your website? What do you show them 30 days after that or six months after that? What are those designs, what are those calls to action, what landing pages do those go to?

And then on the email side, what kind of messages can you send people on an automated basis to generate more sales, and to educate them further along in the process, so that they go from a lead to a customer faster? Or if you're an e-commerce store and they purchase something, what email automation can you send to cross-sell and send them additional ideas for products they might want to buy so as to get more sales out of them? That's called a "twofer" or a "threefer" if they buy one product and you can advertise to them and get them to buy two or three. And boom! You just tripled your return on your investment for your marketing. So, start focusing on how you can use automation to grow your brand.

Question nine is: What content do you need to build, what designs do you need to design, what content do you need on your website, what landing pages do you need to have? Ultimately, what funnels do you need to build? One of those funnels is going to be from your ad copy (or your image ad or your video ad) that leads to a landing page, or may lead to an automated email and a variety of different things. So, what is that funnel? What does the funnel look like? Start to write all that down, get it organized, start writing the content for it, and start designing all the assets.

Question ten, the last question: Who's in charge? Who's responsible for managing all of your marketing, and for holding people accountable for achieving these goals, or holding themselves accountable? Who's going to be the one who is checking and making sure that it's working and making educated decisions and optimizing based on data? What does that look like, and how often are they checking in? Who's responsible for making sure all of this is done so that you can execute the game plan? You need to put somebody in charge, whether it's you, or somebody in your organization, or hiring a company like another marketing company to do these things. You need to have somebody who is an expert, who is a resource, and who is invested in ensuring that the marketing plan that you thought through becomes a reality at the end of the day, and drives the kind of return you're looking for.

8.3 Content Marketing Plan Steps

Steps to Launch Successful Content Marketing Plan

1.   Step number one begins with the end in mind.

You can't reach where you want to go unless you know about where you want to end up. By identifying these goals, you can structure your marketing campaign to help you achieve them. What are you trying to achieve? Do you want to create more leads, make more sales, trying to increase customer satisfaction or engagement with a particular department? Whatever you define as your goals, that's how you can structure your marketing campaign. If you want more leads, that's where your focus should be. If it's sales you're after, you need to invest your efforts there. If you got more than one top priority, you have *zero* top priorities. So narrow it down and focus in on precisely what you're trying to accomplish and that's where you're going to see success. This is also an excellent opportunity to do a SWOT analysis of your business: strengths, opportunities, weaknesses, and threats. Identify what those are and figure out a way that this new marketing campaign can help you overcome those. Do you have a strength that you want to market? Is there a weak point that you, as a business, can address? Is there a threat to your company that you need to focus on? What opportunities do you see to really generate some success?

2. Step number two is setting your timeframe. There is nothing as bad as sitting down and planning out what you desire your marketing strategy to be and then never launching or initializing the process.

By setting a timeframe, start date and a drop-dead date, you're able to work according to your content calendar. Bear in mind; there is an opportunity for failure here. You should never push yourself to the point of producing average content and average results or rushing through the development and design of your ad copy. You should have a gap to change and identify whether there is a need to improve something or not. Identify when you want to launch and get ready to do so, but give yourself some margin just in case things you don't have control over pop up, and you'll be still able to adapt. By doing so, you're able to ensure that you create a great campaign, launch it when necessary, but you've also got some bit of room just in case.

3. Step number three is to know your milestones. Launching a marketing campaign is not easy, so you want to make sure that you've set these milestones and even micro-milestones to determine success as you accomplish it. What kind of targets do you have? Could

you set a milestone for making your initial sale? You can set a benchmark for the initial launch. You can set a benchmark for the initial time that the marketing effort produces good sales. An alternative milestone could be when the first time that the effort pays for itself with money leftover. These are the different ways to know if you're on the right track.

Just launching a marketing campaign in the very beginning does not equal immediate results, so by coming up with these milestones, you can help motivate yourself and inspire your team to see where your growth is coming from and work on that.

4.   Step number four is to identify your budget. You always want to make sure your budget is in check. Start by identifying where you want to spend and how much. This allocates your energies to where they need to be. Knowing the amount of money that you want to invest, the amount of investment that you're playing in these marketing campaigns will help you rest better at night. You need to ensure that any financial resource that you're investing is being used *wisely*. Small business owners need to keep track of where the money they spend is going, so it's not something that you can just

tap into without thinking it through. By figuring out the amount that you want to spend and how much that spending should result in a return on investment will help you determine where you're receiving the best results and to be able to invest that budget on what makes the most sense.

5.   Step number five is to choose your channels. You have to select the channels that you're going to run your marketing campaign on. With so many available to choose from, it's critical to focus on what your actual goals are. Are you going to be selling products? Then you may want to be on Google Shopping. Are you trying to capture more leads and want to focus on intent based search or an inbound search? In that case, perhaps you want to have a campaign running on Google Adwords. Are you producing DIY information, or a lot of great content, copy, images? Well, Pinterest or Instagram may be an excellent option to use. There are several methods that you can run for a campaign, so you have to identify the channels that your consumers are using. Even more so, determine where in the sales funnel they are when they're using those campaigns. Often you can use these different channels to identify the right kind of customer at the right time.

And because you have already decided what your budget is, you know where you can flex and where you can transfer funds to achieve the best result. By understanding your destination, you can create the road to get there. By focusing on the right marketing channels, you're able to reduce any extraneous spend or superfluous spend that you should avoid. So consider your budget, choose your channels wisely, and then optimize.

6.   Step number six is to launch. Now it's time to act on this next step. You've already selected your milestones, you know where you're going, established your goal, planned your budget, and selected your channels. Now it's time to focus on the launch. This can be the scariest part of the process. Up until this point, the steps were all based on theory. You've been choosing what to do and trying to determine where you want to go. Research different tactics and channels that you want to focus on. Now it's time to turn it all on and check the results. If you've done your job well and you've budgeted and acted on it effectively, you'll start to see the data coming in. You'll see clicks, interactions with your ads, comments, conversions, shares, likes, things like that. Review the data, follow up on them,

engage with your audience, and use this to execute your marketing campaigns effectively.

7.   Step number seven is to optimize. All the data are in. You have the clicks, the conversions, all the analytics you can want. Now is the perfect opportunity when you can start to go through and refine your campaign. You can improve the keywords you're focused on, refine your budget, refine the channels, change out ads, reduce or remove the budget for specific campaigns and increase or move it over to other campaigns that are doing well. Take everything that you've learned, everything that you see from this real-world data, and apply it. Everything you've done on paper has led you up to this point. You've focused incredibly hard on ensuring that the campaign you built initially been is as focused and as high-quality as it can be. Now is the time where you use real information to optimize. Don't be afraid to pull down ads. Don't be scared to create new ones or test new things. Don't be afraid to completely abandon channels that are not producing the results you want. Now is the time to work on any adjustments that you want to and then continue making them as you move forward. Find out what works, focus on that, remove what doesn't,

and have a fantastic marketing campaign.

A Perfect Content Marketing Plan

1. Content Audit - The first step in a content marketing plan is to conduct a content audit. To be able to do so, you must collect all the data that your company has. This data is your content which has already been posted on your website or social media outlets. This can be done through a content inventory spreadsheet. This audit will give you an idea about which content has been the most successful and why.

2. Audience Defining - The most crucial step in a content marketing plan is defining the audience. This is the purpose behind your content audit. Even a robust content marketing plan can fail if you don't know for whom you are creating your content. To understand more, dive deeper into the content audit to check which customer responded to what post. You can even create a buyer persona by giving it a name and adding other demographics that you need to target.

3. Match Content with Audience - You need to dive deeper into your content audit to see which content has the most number of responses. Why did that content become popular among your customers?

What message is being delivered through that content? To target the ideal audience for a particular piece of content, make sure the content is informational and compelling for your customers.

4. Create Content Calendar - The next step in a content marketing plan is to create a content calendar. This calendar ensures that you don't miss any content throughout the month. A content calendar has to answer your what, who, when, why, and where about your **content**. Consider, as well, which formats you will be posting your content under in the coming month.

5. Track and Report - The last and vital step in your content marketing plan is to track your content **marketing** success. There are different metrics on which content marketing report can be prepared, such as searches, click-through rate, and so on. Tracking makes it easier to investigate it deeply so that you can change your content marketing plan in the future if needed.

Your Quick Start Action Step:

Schedule in your calendar when the plans outlined in 8.3 will be executed. Add keywords to your content calendar, and schedule your future posts for the best content marketing strategy. You can sign up to Trello right now and see how useful it is to create the perfect content calendar. You can also make changes to your content calendar once you have completed the previous one.

Chapter 9:
How to Measure
Content Marketing
Success

Chapter 9: How to Measure Content Marketing Success

9.1 Measuring Content Marketing Success

Many business owners still find it challenging to keep the business objective under surveillance while starting content marketing. With each creative idea you come up with, ask yourself some questions like, "How will this help meet my audience's objectives? How will this help meet my content marketing objectives? How will this help meet my digital PR objectives, and how it has helped meet my business objectives, providing value to the current and prospective clients?" This should be the aim of any content marketing strategy. Once you get this part, the rest will follow. How can you entertain, inspire, teach, help, or engage your clients or prospective clients? How can you make them want to share your content or spend a lot of time browsing your site? Once you have a few rough ideas of how you'd like to tap into your client's passions, interests, problems, and objectives, you can start getting these ideas through a specific tool to measure content marketing success.

How can this tool help you get the rankings, visibility, and organic traffic that you want from relevant key phrases? How can this content campaign help meet your business goals? Not all content ideas will work for every business, but if you find one that does, you'll come out a winner.

You can measure the amount of success of your content campaign by using audience-based metrics. How many times was your content shared on social media? How many unique page views did you get, and what was the average time on site, and what does that say about the usefulness your content? You can measure social shares with an online tool called Buzzsumo, which gives information about unique page views, and time spent on-site can be found within your Google Analytics. SEO-based metrics, rankings, visibility in search engines, and organic traffic are all perfect metrics for tracking your content marketing success. You can measure rankings and visibility, and organic traffic can be estimated with a well-set-up Google Analytics account. Such tools help you accomplish your business objectives, and a well-set-up Google Analytics account will give you precise information about the way your web visitors navigate your site. All of these metrics can show you that your content marketing strategy has become successful, and your customers are connected to you. You get evidence that your customers trust your brand or your services.

9.2 Importance of Measuring Content Marketing Success

A practical and effective content marketing strategy can take you towards the path to your success. You get connected to your customers at a deeper level. You get to know whether they are satisfied with your content or not. When you don't estimate your success in content marketing, you miss an excellent opportunity to improve your content.

To make useful improvements, you must decide to measure your content marketing success through various metrics. These metrics can be things like searches, time on website, clicks, downloads, and more.

Ten years ago, content marketing was all about impressions and clicks. The content was written for search engines and not for people. That won't work today; search engines are reading semantically and not just keywords, and if you're optimizing towards a click, it only gives you part of the story. Content marketing is about a long-form true value exchange with your consumer.

A click tells you is you've got a good headline, but to be fair measuring past a click can be a challenge. Half of all marketers struggle to measure their content marketing effectiveness. But new metrics are emerging, and engagement metrics are going to replace the simple click for content marketing.

All brands must be able to understand, at a page level, how users are engaging with their content. Things like social sharing, rate of watching the video altogether, bounce rates, dwelling time on page, deeper clicks in the website, all of these metrics are incredibly valuable. Now, these measurements are available, and brands are using multiple tools to get their metrics.

Clever content and smart distribution make measuring marketing success easy. What does success look like for your activity? Is it video views, social shares, the total time spent on the content established?

Planning at this stage is crucial, not when you're launching. The post-campaign analysis is just as critical as pre-campaign planning. It's about articulating what you've already earned from your activity. Did you succeed in your objectives? What are you going to do next? Brand uplift and recall studies would tell you what your engaged users think about your brand. Now, this is where all of the test and content finally pays off. This produces actionable insights to that can be used when crafting every part of your future content marketing strategy.

9.3 Tools to Measure Content Marketing Success

To measure the success of your content marketing, you need to work out what it is you're trying to track. So, set yourself a goal whether it links to content, social shares, revenue traffic, or transactions. Once you've worked this out, it's easier to establish how well your content is performing.

There are many free and paid tools to measure, monitor, and track the success of content marketing:

1. Google Analytics - Google Analytics is a service or a tool offered by Google to perform the analysis of website traffic and traffic sources. This tool helps us in tracking all visitors from all search engines and social networks. It can also help us to monitor advertising,

pay-per-click, email marketing, and links within PDF documents. Along with the other benefits provided by this service, its implementation is also straightforward as you have to own a Google account. Sign in your Google Analytics account and click on "admin" in the menu bar, and then in the account column, select "create a new account" from the dropdown menu. Then click "website" or "mobile app," then set up your account by providing the website name, URL category, etc.

Once you add your site, the next step is to set up the tracking ID. The steps to get this ID are as follows: Sign in your account. Click "admin" from the top menu bar. Then select the property you are working with through the "account and property" column. After this, click "traffic info/code." After finding your traffic code snippet, which contains several JavaScript lines, copy it and then paste it into the header file of the webpage.

This tool is without any fee, it's accessible, easy to use, and it gives you access to a variety of data. Now you can measure the performance of your on-site content so you can find out which pieces are performing well, which ones aren't doing as well and can you change your strategy to bring those pieces in line with the highest performance. You can also look at the bounce rate. So, if you've got a blog, for example, is there a reason why your bounce rate might be high and can you bring this down? You can also look at ROI and transactional data to see how the content is directly impacting the money you make as a business.

2. Buzzsumo - There are free, and premium paid versions of this tool. It doesn't matter which one you've got, but obviously the more you spend, the more you'll get. This tool gives you access to engagement so you can put the domain of your site or your blog straight into the tool and it will show you which of the pieces of content you offer are the strongest-performing ones. It's not based on links; it's based on social media shares. With this tool, you can also look at your backlink data to show where you're getting your links from. For example, if there's a particular piece of content you want to track so you can set up media monitoring, you can do that. You enter your brand name, and it will alert you to show you any external sites that featured you and referenced your branding, which is good when you're looking for coverage. Lastly, there's a cue anchor, so this tool is excellent to show

you the importance of having SEO and content and how well they can work together.

Your Quick Start Action Step:

If you have not registered with these tools, register now and set up your accounts, because it's your right to know what results from your content marketing efforts are paying off.

Chapter 10:
How to Avoid Mistakes in Content Marketing

Chapter 10: How to Avoid Mistakes in Content Marketing

10.1 Content Marketing Mistakes and How to Prevent Doing Them

Long before content marketing became a primary choice among marketers, Bill Gates famously said, "Content is King." Today, the prescience of his what he said is clear. Social media is highly in demand as the internet is being used by everyone. Therefore, no brand can afford to avoid content marketing if they want to build a reputation and increase sales. The issue content marketers face is that it's easy to mess up when creating and sharing content. It's not enough to blindly post content on Facebook and roll the dice--you have to ensure that Facebook is the right channel for what you're promoting and that the content is of interest to your desired audience. Make bad choices, and you could be wasting your marketing budget.

These are the 10 most common content marketing mistakes and how to avoid them:

1. Sharing low-quality content - This might seem

obvious, but the content you share must be high quality and relevant for it to be effective in practical terms. That means you should spend time thinking about which content is most likely to be effective. Be willing to invest in the time and effort to create quality content or pay to an expert to do it for you. Do not share any piece of content without reading or reviewing it yourself. It's not enough to read a headline before sharing an article from an industry publication or blog. Read the whole text first and then add your thoughts before sharing it.

2. Creating unuseful content - Creating or sharing content that isn't useful to your target customer or audience is also a huge mistake. Sharing content that isn't truly relevant to the target audience is bad for business. You may feel tempted to share that cute video of a pup or pet products, but unless you're a veterinarian or a dog groomer, this video will *not* attract your audience. Save that for your personal social media pages, and make sure every piece of content shared by your business affects your customers and their interests.

3. Choosing the wrong platform - Picking the wrong

places to focus your content marketing is about more than just choosing the right content. Your team has to choose the best places to *share* that content. If most of your audience use Twitter, but you're promoting your top content on LinkedIn, you're missing the chance to engage with them. Creating a customer persona and utilizing it to work on your marketing campaigns can help you avoid this mistake. The solution to this mistake is to select two or three specific social media websites. These platforms are where your customers are searching for stuff related to your business so you can get their attention at the right time. If your content is not creating much hype at that platform, consider moving to the next social media website. This technique will save you money, and you can use your marketing budget at a place where it is beneficial.

4. Not building trust and authority - The next common mistake is failing to build trust and credibility via the content you are sharing. Your content is your reflection; it is an extension of who you are. Every time you get connected to your audience through your content, you get an opportunity to establish your brand as a unique identity. However, it's not enough to share content. You should also take a moment to add what

your thoughts on it are, what the writer said, whether there was anything they got wrong or missed. When you integrate your brand into curated content, you build authority.

5. Forgetting the content marketing is a two-way street - When you're marketing your business, you may feel as if you are communicating through a loudspeaker to get the attention of the crowd. This is the wrong analogy. The ideal content marketing is a two-way process. It is a connection and conversation between you and your customers. You don't just want audiences to take in what you're saying; you should want to hear what they have to say too. You can avoid this mistake by creating pathways for customer engagement. For example, ask your customers to share their reviews or experiences after using your service or product. Enable sharing methods for your content so that your audience can share it with their friends, as well. You can also ask questions of your customers through emails, comments, polls, or direct messages. This is done to keep your customers engaged and to be able to react to what you share.

6. Not soliciting and sharing user-generated content -

This mistake is closely aligned with the last one. Not all the content that you share on your content marketing mediums have to be created by you. You should be actively finding out ways to indulge your audience in creating content for you. For example, a tourism company may ask its customers to share pictures of their favorite trips. This is a wonderful way to keep them engaged in conversation.

7. Not utilizing scheduling tools to keep an active presence - How active is your presence on social media? If the answer is "not so much," then you're doing it inaccurately. The whole goal of social media marketing is to maintain an active presence. One all-too-common mistake companies make is not using scheduling tools to help them with social media marketing. A scheduling tool can ensure your posts go out on time even if you get pulled into a crisis at the office. Some social media sites like Facebook have tools allowing you to set up a schedule when to publish a post. However, your best choice is to use content management software to set up a schedule for all of your content so you'll never miss a post.

8. Not asking for what you want - Are you asking your

readers for what you want when you post content? It may sound odd, but if you're not requesting a call to action such as comments, shares or likes, then you're likely not getting the engagement you seek. The only way to influence user action is to ask for it. A lot of businesses will ask their visitors to share their content, and you should do the same.

9. Not varying the format of your content - This one is pervasive in content marketing. You end up sharing the same type of content every time. For example, if you are creating just blog posts, or photographs or videos, then you're missing the best opportunities to get engaged with your customers. One of the benefits of doing content marketing is that it's incredibly versatile. You can start sharing video one day, an infographic the next, and an in-depth think-piece the day after. Avoid falling into a rut and instead, try conceptualizing a content idea in several ways. So instead of posting a blog post about a complicated issue, try hiring a graphic designer to make it into an infographic. Write a story with an accompanying photograph within the text content. As long as you could make a conscious effort to vary your content, you can prevent this mistake.

10. Not refining as you go - The final content marketing mistake on this list is the refusal to refine content and strategies as you go. This can have a negative significance on your return on investment. No marketing campaign is flawless out of the gate. Even marketers with years of experience can misjudge a piece of content and its effect. The key to successful marketing is knowing when something isn't working and then to correct it. You can utilize analytics to learn the performance of your content. The information you collect will help you figure out the type of content that gets the highest levels of engagement and which ones don't impact with your audience. It can also help you pinpoint weaknesses in the marketing strategy of your overall content.

Conclusion

As you have learned, Content Marketing is both an art and a calculation. If you want your content marketing endeavors to be successful, then you should use the content appropriately. Share it where it will be most useful and then measure the results. A business that tries to avoid these mistakes can have the leverage it needs to create a successful engagement with their customers or audience.

Your Quick Start Action Step:

Create an error-free content marketing strategy and avoid mistakes right from the beginning.

Bonus Chapter: Integrating Content Marketing with Social Media Marketing

Bonus Chapter: Integrating Content Marketing with Social Media Marketing

The agenda for perfect content marketing can be improved by adding social media marketing into the mix. Social media marketing is a significant part of content marketing. You should connect your content marketing to social media marketing by adding together the following elements:

1. Buyer Persona - This is the first step to setting up your content and social media marketing strategy. You can create a buyer persona by integrating the necessary qualities of your ideal customer. Usually, a buyer persona is the fictional representation of your target customer. For example, age group, education, occupation, marital status, qualities, hobbies, goals, challenges, and more. Then you can name your buyer persona with a random name. After this, you are all set to target your buyers. For a particular buyer persona, you can create posts related to the challenges and goals of your buyer.

2. Objectives - Suppose your business objective is to generate a specific rate of ROI for the coming month. In this case, your social media marketing objective should be creating posts about corresponding products and generating leads through social media engagements. If your business objective is to create awareness about a product, then your relevant social media marketing objective should be making customers aware through posts concerning that particular product.

3. Products - When you are done setting up the buyer persona and goals, your next step is to consider your product. You need to check how your product fits into the buyer persona. You must keep an eye on how you create content and how you create social media posts, ensuring everything gets aligned. You should create content and posts about the product, offer, event, editorial, and be solution-specific. After creating content, you must focus on the message that is being delivered by your content. Whether it is emotional, monetary, rational, or productive.

4. Plan Editorial Strategy - You can create content ideas through the message you want to deliver. You have to

map the content around the buyer's journey. The editorial content has to be educational and exciting.

5. Content Calendar - Your content and social media calendar should operate side-by-side so that you are working on a particular topic at the same time. The current social media posts must resonate with the content on your blog posts, podcasts, etc. By doing so, you would give a similar message across all of the platforms.

Every company knows how vital it is to have a digital presence, whether it is a Twitter profile, Instagram page, Facebook page, or website. But how does anyone avoid the challenges of the ever-growing digital world if their brand's marketing efforts aren't integrated? Today's customers are intelligent. They know what they expect from online content. They want to get entertained, educated, and informed. They feel connected to content only if it adds value to their day-to-day lives. The formula for joining content with social media marketing is also called integrated digital marketing (IDM). IDM strategy is characterized by defining and establishing your brand in the digital age. Organic search, social channels and paid search are used to promote your brand's message and content effectively. Using paid search tactics such as AdWords from Google will offer your brand numerous ways to micro-target prospects in a more cost-effective manner. Use IDM strategy to educate your customer about your brand. The same message can be conveyed to all platforms at the same time. This can be accomplished regardless of the place or location of the customer. Three factors drive mobile users: convenience, simplicity, and proximity. Create relevance and top-of-mind awareness. The last step in an IDM strategy is to measure and refine your efforts to be successful. You must continually evaluate all tactics to measure your marketing outcomes.

Here are some helpful tips when executing a user-generated marketing strategy:

1.   Tip one: To get users attracted to your content, you should prioritize engaging with them. They must feel appreciated. To do so, you have to encourage them to join the conversation. Know your audience, so you know which themes and subjects fuel their interest and bear that in mind when creating content. In creating a community online, participation only happens when

you create an incentive for doing so. You also should set standards and values that your users should follow and adhere to. Promote this community and always contribute by showing that you have an active voice. Let them be themselves and provide them the freedom to create as they wish.

2.   Tip two: In developing a strategy, you need to have clear goals. Don't go into implementing a user-generated execution without having the right strategy in place. Goals could vary from increasing followers, creating sales, making a topic trend, etc. Defining your goals is crucial so you can easily tailor-fit the type of content you want your users to create. Align these goals to your long-term objectives. User-generated content is a tool to enable you to reach those goals. This form of marketing is only useful if it is the right fit for what you need.

3.   Tip three: Your users should have a definite sense of direction of what to create, whether it's photos or reviews. Without a clear direction, you might be getting in the way of customers' engagement. You need to have some ground rules to protect your content and your viewers. If you don't set such rules, your content

might become prone to trolls.

4.   Tip four: Don't just let your users create content without your permission. You should encourage them to give credit to your content while sharing. In a nutshell, they need to get approval from you before reposting your content. Creating a marketing strategy around user-generated content makes you friendly in the eyes of your customers.

Your Quick Start Action Step:

If you haven't done it already, integrate your content marketing plans with social media marketing. Social Media Marketing helps make your content marketing efforts more effective. The methods and techniques mentioned in this chapter are essential for setting up the perfect content marketing and social media marketing plan.

Check out the author's other book on social media marketing by entering the author's name into the online store's website.

Conclusion

Thank you again for owning this book!

I hope this book was able to help you to understand advanced content marketing methods, and you might have a better picture for your next content marketing strategy. There are many tools and tactics for creating a content marketing plan and make your business a success.

The next step is to use these techniques for your business or client and reap the benefits of content marketing like never before.

Thank you, and good luck!

Bonus Sneak Peek

"Social Media Marketing"

I would like to share with you a Sneak Peek into another book of mine that I think you will enjoy.

The book is called "Social Media Marketing", and it's about marketing your products and services using Social Media. Enjoy this free chapter!

Chapter 6: Social Media Content That Engages

How Social Media Content Can Improve Engagement

Content that engages will not only draw the attention of online users; they will also be interested in reading through the text, regardless of length.

Your content must contain relevant information that is not just about your brand or products to achieve its purpose; it must be of value to the reader, which means that engaging content is a well-researched piece that has beneficial information to your target audience.

There is a feature on most social media platforms that enables you to share content with your friends. One quality of engaging social media content is that it gets a lot of reposts.

It is essential that you carry out a thorough research on topics that are related to your brand, and compose informative articles on these topics. You should ensure that this content is original and engaging to promote your brand and keep your audience on your platform.

Content does encourage responsiveness on your platform and boosts awareness of your brand. Some companies hire professional writers and content developers to create engaging material for their brands to attract and keep customers.

After setting up your social media account, you have to set up a schedule for posting content to encourage engagement. You should be smart about posting content so you don't bore your audience, and that is why you should be creative and innovative with it.

You should post content about different aspects of your niche to ensure that your posts do not become too monotonous or similar. A good way around this is to arrange the content in three to four categories and post them at regular intervals. For example, you could have inspirational content, how-to content, promotional content, and informative content. Arrange it in such a way that it is easy to post them in turns and at regular intervals to keep your content interesting, engaging, and fresh.

Steps for Creating Engaging Content on Social Media

In this section of this book, we are going to guide you on the steps you should take to create engaging content. Quality content is more than just writing and posting articles, images and videos on your social media platforms.

The following are steps on how to create engaging content for your target audience to help grow your business:

1.   Plan Your Content — It takes planning and time to dish out quality content regularly. First, you have to draw up a suitable plan of when to post, what to post, and how to post the content. A plan enables you to stay consistent in your content marketing with social media. With a plan, you will become regular in your posting as you set the number of posts per week and the times to post during the week. Planning involves

searching for the right topics to post and carrying out research on keywords and links to use for your content. The plan may also include designating certain subjects to writers if you have content writers working for you. Planning is the first step in finding success with your social media content marketing.

2.   Research what Content your Target Audience Wants — The next step is to understand what your audience will be interested in, and how it will help you grow your brand. You do not want to waste time and resources on creating content which your audience will not find interesting. While researching suitable, relevant content, you can check up on your competitors and make a note of the articles that have the highest response. You can check out the structures of these posts and use them as a guideline when you post on your social media platforms. Researching also involves studying the articles you intend to post. You research the topic, search for the right keywords to use, and decide what will make up the content of the post. The content of the post may include words, images, and videos as you look for something engaging. This step is crucial in creating an engaging post. The primary research you should do at this stage includes:

○   Topics that your targeted audience will find interesting to increase responses on your post.

○   The actual content that will make up those topics, including images and videos.

○   The best time to post the content on social media platforms to ensure maximum engagement.

3. Create the Content — There is even more to creating engaging content after you have found the right topics and keywords to use. Creating content requires that writers have an understanding of the topics and how to use keywords for search engine optimization. Most brands do pay writers to help them create quality content even after they have researched the right topics and keywords. These writers are professionals, and they know how to input the keywords accurately in the content to ensure the proper keyword density and accurate readability score. All these are geared towards increasing the organic search of the article. In your article, embed social media tools that will enable your post to be shared easily online through the social media shortcuts that you provide in the article. Thus, if you keep search engine optimization in mind when you create your content, your post can be shared easily on these platforms. When these audiences search for your

post online and find it interesting and engaging, they will share it on their social media platforms using the available social media buttons in the article. Moreover, we can see why we need to put a lot of consideration and preparation for creating our article.

4.   Images and Videos for Your Content — Content with pictures and videos have more engagement than content with no images or videos. Images have a way of attracting an audience, especially on platforms like Facebook or Twitter. It is a fact that tweets with images and videos have more clicks than tweets without them. Use high-quality images, which you can find on popular websites for free images. You can find pictures on these websites related to your brand and use them in your content to increase audience interest. You can make use of a smartphone with a high-quality camera to take images of your products or services being offered and post them to engage your audience.

To learn more about this book and how it can help your business, check out "Social Media Marketing" by Gavin Turner.

Bibliography

Cleary, I. (2016, September 26). Content Conversion Funnel: How to Make Sales From Stories. Retrieved from http://www.curata.com/blog/sales-stories-content-conversion-funnel/

Content Marketing Wiki. (2019, February 15). Retrieved April 28, 2019, from https://en.wikipedia.org/wiki/Content_marketing

Developing a Content Strategy. (n.d.). Retrieved from https://contentmarketinginstitute.com/developing-a-strategy/Gotter, A. (2017, July 05). The 8 Main Different Types of Content and How to Use Them. Retrieved from https://adespresso.com/blog/main-different-types-content-use/

McGill, J. (2018, September 04). How to Develop a Content Strategy: A Start-to-Finish Guide. Retrieved from https://blog.hubspot.com/marketing/content-marketing-plan

Patel, N. (n.d.). Content Marketing Made Simple: A Step-by-Step Guide. Retrieved from https://neilpatel.com/what-is-content-marketing/

Siu, E. (2018, September 12). Content Marketing Funnel: When to Use Different Types of Content. Retrieved from https://www.singlegrain.com/blog-posts/content-marketing/content-marketing-funnel-using-different-types-content/

What is Content Marketing? (n.d.). Retrieved from https://contentmarketinginstitute.com/what-is-content-marketing/

www.ingramcontent.com/pod-product-compliance
Lightning Source LLC
LaVergne TN
LVHW022345060326
832902LV00022B/4264